THE $50 WEEKLY SHOP

Jody Allen was made redundant in 2009 while on maternity leave and pregnant with her second child, born 12 months after the first baby. She started her website, Stay at Home Mum, to share her money-saving experiences while her family lived on one wage, and it has since become Australia's biggest mothers' network. Jody now connects with hundreds of thousands of women and has created a successful business. She is also the author of *Once a Month Cooking* and *Live Well on Less*. Jody lives in Gympie, Queensland, with her husband and two boys.

stayathomemum.com.au

*Dedicated to my Dad, Graeme Pickford,
for teaching me the value of money*

Jody Allen

THE STAY AT HOME MUM

THE
$50
WEEKLY
SHOP

HOW TO BUY GROCERIES FOR A FAMILY OF FOUR ON A TIGHT BUDGET

MICHAEL JOSEPH
an imprint of
PENGUIN BOOKS

MICHAEL JOSEPH

UK | USA | Canada | Ireland | Australia
India | New Zealand | South Africa | China

Penguin Books is part of the Penguin Random House group of companies
whose addresses can be found at global.penguinrandomhouse.com.

First published by Penguin Group (Australia), 2017

Text copyright © Jody Allen, 2017

The moral right of the author has been asserted.

Cover design by Louisa Maggio © Penguin Random House Australia Pty Ltd
Text design based on a design by Pauline Haas © Penguin Random House Australia Pty Ltd
Author photograph by Paul Harris
Typeset in Scala by Samantha Jayaweera, Penguin Random House Australia Pty Ltd
Colour separation by Splitting Image Colour Studio, Clayton, Victoria
Printed and bound in Australia by Griffin Press, an accredited ISO AS/NZS 14001
Environmental Management Systems printer.

National Library of Australia
Cataloguing-in-Publication data:

Allen, Jody, author.
The $50 weekly shop / Jody Allen.
9780143797326 (paperback)
Home economics.
Grocery shopping.
Budgets, personal.
Low budget cooking.
Thriftiness.

332.024

penguin.com.au

Contents

Introduction

HI EVERYONE! MY NAME is Jody, and I *love* living frugally – it gives me a real sense of security knowing that I have enough money to pay my bills. But it's important to understand that for me, being frugal doesn't mean being cheap. Being cheap means going without to make your bank balance bigger at the expense of having a good time. To me there's no fun in that! I like a good red wine, I love holidays, I love chocolate and getting my hair done. Being frugal allows me to afford treats like this without going into credit-card debt.

Now I've always been careful with money, but a few years ago, something happened that challenged everything I thought I knew about managing it well. After being made redundant, having two babies in twelve months and living on one income, I did all the sums and worked out that I only had a measly $50 left to spend on groceries. OMG! I was devastated. At that time I had been spending $200 a week on groceries – and I'd thought *that* was pretty good!

I cried for a week. It looked like we were going to lose the house we'd worked so desperately hard to buy. But sometimes you just need to feel sorry for yourself for a bit before you pick yourself up, dust yourself off and decide to damn-well do something about it. And that's exactly what I did!

I was determined that we would somehow manage on $50 a week. So, like I would with any goal, I broke it down into manageable steps. In the first week my goal was to spend $150 on groceries instead of $200. And to my surprise, it was pretty easy! I felt really good about making a bit of progress, so the next week I aimed for $100. To be honest, that was a lot harder, but I was just *so* determined – there was no way we were going to lose the house! Plus, it was a challenge, and kind of satisfying in a way. So I kept going, gradually reducing the weekly amount until I got it down to $50. And that's how we lived for four years.

I learned so much from that experience that in January 2011 I started the website Stay at Home Mum to share both my own and my community's wonderful money-saving ideas. Sure it took me a couple of years to get it right, but the important thing was that I saved a lot of money, ate really well, fed my family – and kept the house!

If you're not convinced that frugality is a good idea, consider this: Australia has become one of the world's most expensive countries to live in. According to Numbeo, rent in Australia is 7.5 per cent higher than in the United States and the cost of living is 8 per cent higher.

And there's this scary statistic: in 1970 the average house price was twice the average annual income, while these days average house prices are seven times our annual income. And if you live in Sydney – make that *ten times* your annual income! This means that if you live in Sydney, Melbourne, Perth, Canberra, Brisbane, Newcastle, Adelaide, Wollongong, the Gold Coast or Hobart, there is a good chance you are spending more than one third of your pay packet on rent or your mortgage each week!

Aside from the high cost of living, there are heaps of other reasons why saving money on your food bills is a good idea. For example, you may be:

- cash-strapped due to a load of other bills arriving at the same time
- saving for a deposit on a house
- trying to reduce your credit-card debt

- saving for a trip of a lifetime
- creating a safety net in case you lose your job
- saving for retirement.

But even if none of the above apply to you, it is just smart to live a frugal life. And it reduces stress. Imagine not having to worry about how to pay your next bill because you've already budgeted for it. Plus, being frugal is also very environmentally friendly – we buy only what we need and there's virtually nothing wasted since we repurpose leftovers instead of throwing them out.

After paying your rent or mortgage, food is your next biggest household expense. But it is a 'fluid' cost – one week it might be $200, the next week $180 – so it's a place where you can really pull your belt in and save lots of money.

Now when I say $50 a week, I mean $50 worth of groceries (food), not cleaning items, medicines or appliances. And if you have little children, it doesn't include milk. (When my kids were young we went through 3 litres a day!) The $50 is purely for the food you need for breakfast, snacks, lunch and dinner for one week.

Of course, if you need to buy baby formula or you have five teenage sons, a $50 budget isn't going to work for you, but the principles I share with you in this book will still be incredibly useful for helping you to cut down your grocery bills.

Lots of people assume that eating cheaply has to be unhealthy because of the focus on inexpensive carbs like pasta and rice, but this is not true. While I do include a fair few carbs in my meal plans, I always recommend the wholegrain versions, and balance those with loads of fresh or frozen vegetables along with cheaper proteins such as lentils, beans and eggs. Also, buying fresh fruit and vegetables that are in season is always going to be cheaper, as they are more plentiful and therefore in less demand.

I get super annoyed when people say, 'It can't be done' or 'It isn't healthy or good for you' or 'It's impossible for a family with food intolerances'. I've heard all of these excuses before, and the truth is that you *can* feed a family of four on $50 a week – you just have to be committed to your goal. I know it because I lived it for four years. Am I healthy? Hell, yeah! I'm probably in the best shape I've ever been. Plus my kids are healthy and happy. And I sleep well at night knowing I can pay my bills.

So if you think you want to give it a go, I'm here for you. Let's do this together. This book has all the information you need to set up a frugal kitchen, including more than 200 simple and delicious recipes to keep everyone healthy and happy, along with loads of hacks on the best ways to shop, store and repurpose foods. Plus, you can share your experiences with me and other like-minded people on my website stayathomemum.com.au. We're here to support you.

I wish you all the best.

YOU CAN DO IT!

Jody

CHAPTER 1:
Setting your goal

ALTHOUGH I CALLED THIS book *The $50 Weekly Shop*, the $50 is really only a guide. Every family is different, and it may be that your goal will be to spend less than that, or more than that, depending on your circumstances. When I first did this, my two sons were toddlers so had smaller appetites and different tastes to the ones they have now. Your family will have individual needs, too, so don't beat yourself up if you can't get your food bill down to $50 – the idea is to save money, and how easily you do that will depend on the number of children in your care, their ages, their activity levels, whether you are a sole parent or have a partner, whether you have vegetarians in your family, where you live, etc.

I live in a rural area – in Gympie to be exact. And it is a fairly cheap place to live. I have access to the local markets and can buy produce direct from nearby farmers. If you live in the city you may have to drive a bit further to get good deals on produce, but you also have the great advantage of home delivery – so do your research to find the best deals. Check locally to see if there is a veggie co-op you can join, where you buy bulk produce and share the costs of delivery.

How much are you spending?

The first thing you need to do is to work out how much you are currently spending on groceries. Grab your receipts for the past couple of weeks, sit down and add up all of the food items you've paid for, including takeaway lunches, dinners, snacks, drinks, etc. and work out what you spend on average. If you don't have any receipts, then just do your normal grocery shopping for the first week and keep receipts for every food item you buy (including takeaway). Don't try to save money or do anything out of the ordinary – just shop as you usually would.

Before I began living frugally, I would just 'throw' things in the trolley with a vague plan about what I might do with them – I didn't even bother looking at the price.

When you look closely at the receipts and actually see how much particular items cost, it can sometimes give you that extra jolt you need to keep track of where your hard-earned money is going. But again, please don't despair or feel like the world's biggest tool – everything is fixable.

So how much are you spending? Is this an average week for you?

Now work out what you would ideally like to spend on your weekly grocery bill, given other financial commitments and whatever you are saving money for. If that figure looks scary, don't panic! I didn't do it overnight, and I don't expect you to either. You just need to break it down and do it step by step. That's what will get you there. That's how you get anywhere!

If you are spending $200-plus *just* on food per week, aim to spend 10–15 per cent less for the next shop. How you do this is really up to you, but in this chapter I suggest some simple but effective ways to reduce your spending, including giving up takeaway food, avoiding readymade meals, buying generic-brand staples and avoiding fancy value foods.

Once you've followed those basic principles for a couple of weeks, you'll have the confidence to bring out the big guns – planning your meals, shopping for the best deals, reusing leftovers, making your own staples, growing your own food – all of which will help you reduce your spending until you reach your goal.

Give up takeaway food

I have to be blunt with you – you'll never save money if you buy food that someone else has cooked. End of story. For some people, the idea of having to spend more time in the kitchen is quite scary – we're so used to having fast-food giants on every corner, and aisles and aisles of packaged meals in our supermarkets. And I totally get why we succumb. When we're knackered and have to pick up the kids from sport or music or whatever, it's so tempting to pop into a takeaway place on our way home. But I can tell you from experience that this is where you are *really* wasting your money. I kept all of my takeaway receipts for a year and when I added them up it was truly frightening. The average burger, drinks and chips for the four of us was nearly $40! And we were doing this at *least* twice a week, and then having the occasional takeaway breakfast when we were driving somewhere on the weekends.

Plus, all that takeaway food was expanding our waistlines (especially mine!), so there was the added cost of having to buy new clothes, as well as the incalculable long-term cost to our health.

If you are the kind of family who only has takeaway as an occasional treat, then this part will be really easy. However, if you are having it more than a couple of times a week (and I'm including takeaway breakfast, lunch and dinner here), then it's going to be a bit more of a challenge. But please don't be too hard on yourself. You are changing habits that you've built up over a lifetime, so give yourself a break. If it's too hard to ditch takeaway all at once, then wean yourself off slowly. Reduce it down by one meal a week, or whatever works for you.

To make this step easier, make sure that you have some soups, casseroles, pasta sauces and other premade dishes in your fridge or freezer to help you resist temptation. Here are some of the easiest recipes to consider cooking up on weekends so that they're ready to go during those first few weeks:

- Traditional Spaghetti Bolognaise (page 248)
- Porcupine Meatballs (page 247)
- Super Healthy Chicken Meatloaf (page 258)
- Sausage Risotto (page 236)
- Slow-cooker Pea and Ham Soup (page 169)
- Cream of Pumpkin Soup (page 176)
- Slow-cooker Beef and Barley Soup (page 178)

DANETTE'S STORY

I never chose to be a single mum. When it became the three of us, we were going great for a while, until my savings dried up. I had to make the choice: do I want to move back to the 'safety net' of my mum's house or do I want to grab this situation by the balls and take control of my kids and my life?

When my partner left, he didn't just take his belongings and go, he left unpaid bills that I had no choice but to pay off if I wanted to avoid a black mark against my name.

I decided that I didn't want to run home, I wanted to remain independent and work my way out of this horrible mess. So I sat down and worked out a budget that I could stick to. I broke all of my regular household bills into fortnightly repayments and with what was left, which wasn't much, I had to work out a way to pay back all of my ex-partner's bills and purchase food.

Meal planning became a lifesaver for me. I just had to work out the ingredients I needed each week and to purchase only those items. It saved me from wasting food and buying things I didn't need.

Rent, electricity, car (rego, insurance and maintenance), phone, childcare, school fees, and contents insurance took a huge chunk out of my income, in some ways the universe was working for me and in other ways it wasn't. One bill that Mr Ex left us was not mine – it was paying off a big TV. I just did the most logical thing I could do at the time and called the company up and explained my situation. They were completely understanding and didn't hesitate to come and collect it. (I didn't need one of those huge TVs I was happy with the old one.)

I did the same with other businesses to which my Mr Ex owed money. I explained my situation, told them how much I could afford and then we worked out a payment plan so that I could pay back the debt.

I was left with $60 a week for food. With meal planning, even though we had just the basics we never starved. I became creative with food. I froze leftovers for those days that I just couldn't be bothered cooking and I baked cakes and biscuits instead of buying them all the time. Over time those extra bills were paid out.

The day that I made the last repayment was like the best day of my life. Straight away I started saving the extra money so that I could pay cash for new household goodies. The first item I bought was a washing machine – it felt so good walking away with it and not having a bill to pay off!

My kids don't have the latest gadgets or the trendiest clothes, but they are clothed, they have toys, they have food to eat every day, they have a holiday at Christmas time with the rest of my family and most of all they have a mummy that loves them more than life itself. What more could they ask for?!

Avoid packaged meals and readymade food

Once you've stopped buying takeaway food, it will give you that little boost of confidence you need to take the next step, which is to stop buying readymade meals or partly processed ingredients. The simple reason is that's you are paying *a lot* more for something you can easily do yourself, and it really adds up.

Some of the most expensive readymade foods include:

- sugary breakfast cereals (everything except rolled oats, puffed rice and Weet-Bix)
- sausage rolls, pies, pizzas, frozen lasagne, etc., unless they are super cheap!
- biscuits, cakes, frozen desserts, etc.
- stir-fry and pasta sauces in jars or packets
- pre-cut vegetables and salads (you're paying up to $25 a kg more, depending on the ingredients)
- dips, and grated and sliced cheese
- pre-made chips and nuggets
- meatballs, marinated chicken pieces, crumbed meats, stuffed roasts.

Ditch the 'fancy value' foods

'Fancy value' is the name I give for anything with the words 'gourmet' or 'organic' on the label, or any luxury ingredient that inflates the price. Now, I do value organic foods, and I love that some people work hard to produce them, but I would never buy them from a supermarket. If you want to buy organic fruit and veg, go to a farmers' market or a local grocer and buy the real deal. (The smaller organic farmers often can't afford to pay the exorbitant costs for certification, but that doesn't mean their produce isn't nutritious and delicious!) Also, I hate to be the bearer of bad news, but research has shown that organic fruit and veg is no healthier than standard fruit and veg. What's way more important is whether or not you are eating *enough* vegetables and fruit.

Here are some examples of fancy value foods and what you can use to replace them:

- Spicy chorizo: just buy plain salami – when you cook it no one can tell the difference.
- Double cream: just buy cream and whip it!
- Grain bread with pumpkin seeds: make your own bread with a breadmaker.
- Any cheese except cheddar and cheap parmesan: and yes, mozzarella and other cheeses do taste better (I'm a total cheese buff), but forget about them for this challenge!

Buy generic-brand staples

Buying generic brands is a key principle of the $50 weekly shop challenge. In the past, people tended to look down on generic products. Thank goodness times have changed. We all want quality at a good price, and generic brands are usually 15–25 per cent cheaper than the branded items. Many generic-brand staples (flour, sugar, oats, etc.) are made in the same factories as the branded ones and contain the same ingredients, though this doesn't apply to processed foods such as biscuits, cakes, pies, pizzas, etc. which are not only unnecessary, but usually don't taste anywhere near as good as the real deal.

Sometimes it's hard to choose between the generic and the name brand, even for staple items. We might feel attracted to pretty colours or cute images on the packaging, or we might like the idea that our favourite celebrity uses the same item. Or we might be swayed by words like 'organic' or 'low fat' or 'gluten free'.

Each supermarket chain has its own generic brand, but I personally prefer Black & Gold from IGA. The only way to find the one you like is to try them all.

10 items that you should always buy generic:

1. Olive oil
2. Flour
3. Sugar
4. Butter
5. Milk
6. Cheese
7. Tinned tomatoes and beans
8. Frozen vegetables
9. Cereal and grain products (oats, puffed rice, etc.)
10. Fresh fruit and vegetables

Frugal staples

A well-stocked fridge and pantry means there is always something to eat. If you see any of these items on special, make sure you snap them up!

Rice: There are so many different types – jasmine, basmati, arborio, but brown rice is less processed than white, so has lots more nutrients and fibre. It also has a sweeter, nuttier flavour and a great crunchy texture. Use it instead of white varieties whenever you can. It's a great way to 'stretch' a meal – add a cup of cooked brown rice to a bolognaise sauce or a meatloaf.

Flour: Another staple with a good shelf life, make sure you have self-raising, plain and wholemeal or wholegrain flour. (Note that anything labelled 'whole-wheat' flour is more processed than wholemeal/wholegrain flour because the germ, bran and endosperm are first separated and then recombined.)

Oats: Oats are high in fibre and low in fat and are reputed to lower cholesterol. You can get three kinds of oats: ordinary oats (which have been steamed, rolled and lightly toasted); quick oats (which are the same as ordinary oats but chopped up smaller to make the cooking process faster) and steel-cut oats (also known as pinhead oats or coarse oatmeal). Steel-cut oats are made from whole grains ('groats'), which are chopped into two or three pieces rather than being steamed and flattened, and therefore contain a lot more nutrients. I really like the texture of them compared to the usual rolled oats – they're heartier! Most people think oats are only good for porridge and muesli, but they are also fantastic for baking muffins, slices and bread. And if you give them a whizz in the food processor you can use them to crumb meats, bulk up a rissole recipe, or even add them to smoothies. My favourite way to eat them is in Good Ol' Porridge (page 114).

Pasta and rice noodles: Pasta is so cheap – often less than 50 cents a packet! Include a variety in your pantry: spaghetti, penne, macaroni and lasagne sheets are all good options. Rice noodles are great for the gluten-intolerant – I like vermicelli and the flat noodles, too.

Potatoes: Buy unwashed potatoes. They're not only cheaper but also more nutritious than their fancy washed counterparts. Better still, buy sweet potatoes – these are often similarly priced and contain loads of fibre, vitamin A and potassium. I love sweet potatoes baked in chilli oil and stuffed with beans and cheese (see recipe on page 201)!

Olive oil: I like to buy olive oil in bulk and sometimes I flavour it before using it in cooking. I literally just add a little chilli, garlic or lemon.

Onions: If you buy onions in bulk they can go bad in the cupboard (especially in hot climates!). So why not peel, chop and freeze them in serving-size zip-lock bags. They will last for ages!

Crushed garlic (in a jar): Crushed garlic is so cheap – I've seen it for under $1.50 a jar – and it lasts for a couple of months in the fridge.

Eggs: While they might seem expensive, eggs are actually cheap as far as a good protein goes. I try not to buy mine from the supermarket as I like to know that the chickens who laid them are loved, happy and healthy – their eggs are always so 'buttery' and delicious. So if you can find someone with their own chickens, beg, borrow and steal for their eggs! One of my favourite ways to eat eggs is to serve them scrambled on a freshly made tortilla (page 92) with a little pesto sauce (page 88).

Frozen vegetables: The great thing about frozen veggies, apart from convenience, is that you avoid waste. Nutrition experts reckon that frozen vegetables are just as nutritious as fresh ones (though obviously less tasty). Apparently it's the way you cook veggies, rather than whether they are fresh or frozen, that determines how nutritious they are. Boiling them to death in a big pot of water is out!

Puff pastry: While it's really easy to make homemade shortcrust pastry, puff pastry is way too time-consuming (and difficult). Keep puff pastry sealed in a container in the freezer and it will last for months. I've included some great puff pastry recipes in the book. See my Easy Sausage Rolls (page 146), my Cheesy Beef Puffs (page 153) and my Pizza Pinwheels (page 163). It is one pre-prepared food that is an exception to the rule!

Dry yeast: Dry yeast is great for making homemade bread rolls (page 91), English muffins (page 94), crumpets (page 95) and naan bread (page 96; which also happens to be perfect for pizzas). Buy dry yeast in small quantities as it has a relatively short shelf life.

Cocoa: When you're baking, cocoa is so much cheaper to use than cooking chocolate, but has all the richness and taste. Try my Frugal Chocolate Cake recipe (page 283).

Canned tuna: Tuna is cheap and a great way to get some healthy omega-3s into your diet. The key to serving tuna is to add a distinctive flavour to really make it shine. Tuna goes well with dill, pepper, lemon and chilli. I do love a good Tuna Melt (page 152). It's also delicious stirred through freshly cooked pasta with some black olives and anchovies.

Canned tomatoes: These are an absolute must in any pantry. Grab either the Italian brands (best tomatoes in the world) or the generic brands. Available for as little as 50c a tin, you can buy them whole peeled, chopped, crushed or pureed. They are great to use in soups, casseroles and, of course, delicious pasta sauces. My favourite tomato dish? Good old fashioned spag bol.

Canned beans: Baked beans are very good for your heart, especially if you make them yourself (see recipe on page 138). They're great served on toast for breakfast, in pita bread with some salad for lunch, or as a side dish for dinner. Baked beans are usually made with haricot beans (also called navy beans) and like other legumes (e.g. red kidney beans, chickpeas, lentils) are among the cheapest protein sources on the planet. They also contain iron, folate and loads of fibre. I must admit I've only discovered lentils in the last few years. I like to add a can to my mince dishes to make them go further (the hubby and kids don't even notice!).

Tomato paste: Tomato paste isn't just for homemade pizza, it's also brilliant for adding flavour and richness to most casseroles and is a good substitute for tinned tomatoes in recipes.

Stock cubes: I like to make my own homemade stock from leftover bones (page 102) but I always have a stash of chicken, beef or vegetable stock cubes for adding flavour to soups, stir-fries and casseroles.

Seasonal fruit: Buying only fruit that is in season ensures that you get the best value for money, plus it always tastes better. For example, bananas in season are not only super good for you, but are cheap and filling. I love a few slices of banana with pancakes, or on top of toast with peanut butter (yum!). Bananas are a great source of fibre, potassium and manganese. I also love citrus fruits (lemons, limes and oranges). You can freeze the juice and zest when they're cheap so you can enjoy them in dressings, dips and other recipes all year round.

Seasonal vegetables: These are way cheaper and much tastier than veggies that are out of season. Why not grow your own? Cherry tomatoes are really easy to grow and taste so yummy. This year I tried growing potatoes for the first time and they were absolutely delicious, and the kids loved digging for them every afternoon to include with dinner. Other vegetables that are easy to grow include broccoli, pumpkin and peas. (See more about growing food in chapter 5.)

Dried fruit: I like to keep dried fruit (sultanas, apricots, dates) in the pantry for baking and for snacks.

Bottled sauces: Soy, barbecue, tomato and sweet chilli sauce are all staples I like to keep at the ready. I've included recipes for making your own tomato and sweet chilli sauce too, which can be a super cheap option if you grow your own tomatoes or get a box in season.

Honey: This is often expensive when bought directly from the supermarket – see if you can pick it up at from a farmers' market or local producer.

Butter: I buy the generic brands and freeze them in their packets. Butter is *way* better than margarine – I can't imagine life without it!

Powdered milk and evaporated milk: Good to have these in the cupboard for when you run out of milk and need some for a recipe, or there's a blackout or a zombie apocalypse. Evaporated milk makes homemade coffee taste awesome and is a cheap substitute for cream.

Yoghurt: Buying yoghurt in bulk or making your own means yoghurt is quite cheap (see my recipe on page 97). It is *super* good for you, can be served either savoury or sweet, and freezes really well. I love to eat it plain with a few slices of banana and a handful of dried fruit and nuts stirred through it.

Sugar: I always have some to hand for baking. If you are trying to cut down on white sugar, try replacing it with apple puree in sweet dishes such as cakes and muffins.

SUSANNAH G'S STORY

My husband left me and my baby son two years ago – just walked right out. I haven't seen or heard from him since. Looking back, I think he had a gambling problem (the phone statements kept coming to my house). He was the only one who had access to our bank accounts – I was 18 at the time and didn't have much experience in the world, so I just let him take care of it all. But boy did I have to grow up fast.

All of a sudden I had a six-month-old baby, no husband, no income and rent to pay. The property manager came around quick smart to tell me no rent had been paid. I'm lucky she was really understanding. Luckily the property was in my husband's name so they are chasing him for the money.

I moved back in with my parents and tried to sort things out financially. The first thing I did was to open a bank account – my own bank account. I went and saw Centrelink, who were great, so I had a little money coming in to take care of us.

Next I went out and started to stack shelves at the local supermarket at night – Mum and Dad looked after my son while I worked. After a few months I saved up enough money to buy a small car so I could start looking for a better job.

Soon my son and I could afford to rent a small one bedroom apartment. It was tiny, but it was all ours. It was then that I realised just how many bills I had to pay: car insurance, electricity, phone and internet, etc. Plus food on top of all that. I wish I'd learned about all these types of living expenses at school – I really had no idea.

I'm glad I found out about the $50 shop – it taught me how to cook really easy meals that don't cost a fortune.

I'm really standing on my own two feet now. I have an emergency fund in case anything goes wrong and I'm studying to become a medical secretary – something I've always wanted to do.

Things do go wrong in life, but it's how you handle it that really matters.

Other nifty ways to save money

DRINKS

Kids don't need cordial, fruit juices or soft drinks. Nor do they need premixed chocolate drinks or flavoured straws. Water is a perfectly acceptable liquid to consume – and it's good for you. The kids can drink water at school, too. There is nothing set in stone to say you have to give them 'organic sugar-free juice' which costs an arm and a leg. They're better off with fresh fruit, anyway, as they get the benefit of the fibre as well. If they need a special drink, make them a Milo or a banana smoothie at home.

If you are a tea drinker, buy leaf tea. It is cheaper than tea bags, goes further and making tea in a teapot just like Nanna used to is a really lovely way to serve it – and I think it tastes better!

When you're on the go, take some green tea bags with you in a zip-lock. Green tea is not only good for you, it is much cheaper than buying a tea or coffee from a cafe, which can be $5 a pop! When you feel desperate for a caffeine hit, get a cup of boiling water instead and enjoy your green tea, knowing you've just saved yourself $5 and will be doing your body good!

If you drink coffee, either buy the beans in bulk and grind them as you need them (keep the beans in the freezer). Or, just go instant (if that isn't sacrilege to you . . .).

Always carry your own water bottle in the car and your bag. Never buy bottled water – it is expensive and all that plastic is bad for the environment. You are better off spending that money on a good-quality drink bottle that will last for years!

BREAD

There is nothing in the world like fresh bread, and yes I do make my own because I have a breadmaker and the mix works out way cheaper ($1.30 per loaf). Plus it tastes so amazing that I can't go back to factory-made bread. But if you don't have time for that, generic brands of white bread can be picked up for under $1 a loaf, though they are lower in fibre and nutrients than multigrain and wholemeal versions. Also, don't discount buying day-old bread. Not only is it next to half the price, you can freeze it and it will still be nice enough for making toast, sandwiches, breadcrumbs and things like Slow-cooker Bread and Butter Pudding (page 310).

If your family eats a lot of bread (more than a loaf a day), consider buying a breadmaker. It literally take 30 seconds to put the premade mix in the machine. I do it every night before bed and wake up to a fresh, delicious, ready-to-slice loaf in the morning.

MILK

For the frugal, milk is as cheap as it has ever been, in fact it is cheaper now to buy 2 litres of milk than it is to buy 2 litres of water.

If you are really strapped for cash, and it is all you can afford, buy the cheaper supermarket-branded milk, feed your family and don't feel guilty about it.

If you can afford a little more, please support your local dairy farmers and buy branded milk (there's a greater chance that the processors will pay farmers more for their milk). Even better, try to find a dairy relatively close to where you live (if you can) and buy their milk. Support our Aussie farmers.

Another very economical option if you don't have access to fresh milk every day is to use powdered milk. Of course it doesn't taste as good as the real thing, but it's still a great source of protein, calcium and vitamin D. It's also good to use for baking when the taste doesn't matter so much.

As an aside, I always buy full-fat milk because it tastes better. Good old-fashioned milk isn't going to make us fat – it's more likely to be the amount of sugar we're eating! So if you want milk, buy the real stuff.

MEAT

Meat is notoriously expensive, so if you're serious about saving money, you're going to have to forget rib fillet, scotch fillet, lamb cutlets, etc. But this doesn't mean you'll be eating 'prison slop'. There are loads of cuts of meats that are reasonably cheap to buy. Here is a list of what to look out for.

Minced meat: If you have mince in the freezer, you'll always be able to prepare something for dinner! Beef, pork, turkey and chicken mince each have their own unique taste. I like to buy my mince in bulk at places such as Aldi or Costco and then separate it into family meal sized portions (about 500 g) and freeze them right away (page 241). Never freeze mince in huge lumps, unless you're cooking for a party or you don't mind eating the same dish every night for a week!

Personally I'm a big fan of chicken mince – it doesn't have a strong flavour, so is versatile to use for any dish – I always have a few 500 g lots in my freezer. Note that turkey mince, while low in fat, can be very dry so be mindful of that when you use it for cooking.

Sausage meat: Sausage meat can be purchased in 500 g lots for about $2 – making it very cheap. It is good for Easy Sausage Rolls (page 146) or Meatballs (page 247). It can be very fatty, though, so use it sparingly. I like to form it into patties and cook it on a grill so the fat drips off.

Sausages: Sausages are amazingly versatile. I cut them up and cook them as 'meatballs'. I also cook them whole, then slice them in half lengthways, stuff them with mashed potato and top with cheese. They can also be devilled, curried, wrapped in pastry or baked in casseroles – see my Sausage Stroganoff (page 235). There's a huge variety of sausages available. I buy mine from the butcher instead of the supermarket, as the price is about the same but they taste much better than mass-produced supermarket snags.

Chicken pieces: Back when I was growing up, there was no such thing as chicken breasts. You bought whole chickens or chicken pieces. These days, a lot of people are reluctant to buy chicken on the bone. However, it is not only cheap to buy (especially chicken wings, which are delicious baked with soy sauce and honey) but also far more nutritious than muscle meat. Plus, chicken on the bone tastes better!

You can often buy whole generic brand chickens from as little as $5. Sure, they aren't huge, but I bring them home and cut them up into chicken pieces and they will easily feed a family for two or three meals if you stretch it right!

Gravy beef: Give me gravy beef over rib fillets any day! It used to be considered the 'rubbish' of meat varieties, but now it isn't really that cheap to buy (people have caught on to how delicious it is!). Gravy beef is from the beef shin. It does contain a bit of fat, but it has so much flavour. It needs to be cooked slow and steady. If you want the best beef casserole of your entire life, use gravy beef!

Lamb forequarter chops: These are cut from the lamb's shoulder and are still a relatively good price (compared to the delicious but unbelievably expensive lamb cutlets).

If you have time, remove the meat from the bone before cooking and use it to make Shepherd's Pie (page 249). Or just barbecue the chops as is – totes delish!

Beef chuck steak: Chuck steak is from the neck region and needs to be slow-cooked to break down the connective tissue, or it is tough and inedible. It is more widely available than gravy beef, and works in a similar fashion, but without as much fat content.

Corned beef: This pickled meat may seem expensive, but it can go a long way. Cook it in the slow-cooker and serve it with white sauce and vegetables. The next day, serve it thinly sliced on fresh bread with cheese and mustard pickles. Then, on another night, serve the leftovers in Corned Beef Fritters (page 191) – always a family favourite.

Bacon: Budget bacon can be picked up for as little as $5 a kilo, especially the generic brands. Bacon adds flavour to everything, and is a key ingredient in Impossible Pizza (page 185), Zucchini Slice (page 184), Fried Rice (page 182) and Frugal Carbonara (page 228). When in doubt, add bacon!

DRESSINGS, GRAVY, SAUCES AND DIPS

Once you discover how easy (and cheap) it is to make your own mayo and salad dressings (pages 80–82), you'll never buy them again. And you'll never waste money by throwing out all those jars and bottles that collect at the back of the fridge with expired use-by dates! You won't buy gravy or sauce mixes, either, as I'll show you how to make your own (pages 82–90).

CLARISSA'S STORY

Money is always tight for me and my family. I'm a single mum and I have four kids to feed. There isn't much left over for luxuries, but I still think we eat quite well. I'll often buy a cold cooked chicken – at the big supermarkets you can buy them cheap the next day or I just ask for a cold one and they grab them from out the back. Sometimes I can get them as low as $4! I shred the chicken and use it for sandwiches and salads and loads of other dishes. I also use the bones to make stock in my slow cooker.

We like to eat a lot of soups, as they are cheap and filling. I also sometimes find that buying frozen vegetables works out cheaper for me. I really like spinach and I buy the frozen stuff and use it in all my food. I eat a lot of pasta and rice and like to have at least three days a week that we don't eat meat.

I've gotten to know my local grocer well. He will keep aside the fruit and vegetables that are slightly damaged or unsellable and will give me a whole box for just a few dollars. It really makes a big difference that I can feed my kids some fresh produce and they have fruit for school.

I use my slow cooker a lot. It's cheaper to run than the stove or microwave oven. I picked one up cheap from eBay and it has been a life saver. I'd love to get another one!

I don't think you need a lot of money to feed your family well. I think you just need to think outside the square a little.

Staying motivated

The great thing about the $50 weekly shop challenge is that you can't mess it up – every dollar you save on groceries is a success. And really, the most important factor is your mindset. If you really want to do to it, you will.

Here are some of the ways I kept myself motivated – they might work for you.

TAKING FIVE MINUTES EVERY NIGHT TO PREPARE FOR THE NEXT DAY

The kids are in bed, you've had your cup of tea and a biscuit. Before you go to bed at night – if you can – think about what you may want for dinner the next night.

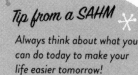

Tip from a SAHM

Always think about what you can do today to make your life easier tomorrow!

Take the meat or meal out of the freezer and place it on a plate in the fridge.

This has so many advantages:

- There's no need to use the microwave, which adds to your energy bill and cooks food unevenly (it can sometimes overcook sections of your meat, making it rubbery and awful).
- You will have your meal ready to be reheated or your meat or other ingredients ready for cooking.
- You have a better chance of sticking to your $50 budget, because once you have thawed that meal/meat, you won't want to waste it. (Whereas, if you'd come home from work and had to defrost something for 15 minutes in the microwave before you could start cooking, there's a greater risk you'd give up and reach for the takeaway brochures.)

KEEP A RECORD OF YOUR SHOP TOTALS

I know it sounds nerdy, but I really liked doing this! I used some graph paper and plotted the total of each shop over a few months and kept it on the fridge. I saw that graph every time I opened the fridge (and apparently the average person opens their fridge 50 times per day!).

TREAT YOURSELF

Like with any goal, I find that if I can look forward to some kind of reward at the end, it keeps me going. When I first did the $50 weekly shop challenge, I used Cherry Ripes as my reward, so if I got to $50, I'd buy one – then eat it after the kids had gone to bed (toddlers don't need chocolate!). It was something I really looked forward to – and even though it was only a very small treat, I cherished every bite!

So use whatever small treat or incentive you like to keep you going. It might be, 'If I get my shopping down to $100 this week, I'll get my nails done' – whatever floats your boat. Of course, don't make the incentive so expensive that you undo all the hard work you've just put into saving money!

FOCUS ON YOUR LONG-TERM GOALS

If you are doing the $50 weekly shop challenge for a longer-term goal, such as saving up for a holiday, a car, elective surgery (!) or some other specific goal, keep a picture of what you are trying to achieve where you will see it every single day. For me the fridge is perfect, but you might prefer your bedroom mirror or some other location.

'NO FOOD SHOPPING FOR A MONTH' CHALLENGE

Recently I tried a 'No food shopping for a month' challenge. I did this because my shopping balance had gotten out of control for a bit. (Yes, even I fall off the wagon!) So I used up everything in my pantry, fridge, freezer and garden, only buying fresh milk, bread mix, and the occasional veggie that was pivotal to a recipe (but I didn't have it in the garden or freezer). I thought that was pretty good. And I tell you what, you certainly learn how to be creative when you only use what you have. I came up with some terrific recipes, and some awful ones. (One turned out like dog food. Sookie and Bella loved it!)

EMILY'S STORY

As a busy mum, feeding a family of six can sometimes get difficult, especially with everyone having different tastebuds. I try to explain to my kids that I can't always make their favourite meals and if they don't like what's being served there's always eggs on toast!

I love to cook and create new dishes, but it does get costly, especially with so many mouths to feed. I find the best way to cut costs is by not wasting ingredients, and I've learned a few tricks to help avoid food wastage.

When bananas are overripe and the kids won't eat them, I peel off the brown skins and freeze the bananas in zip-lock bags. Frozen bananas are great for making smoothies, banana muffins or cakes.

If I have to buy a whole bunch of a particular herb even though I'm only using a small portion, I place the rest in a zip-lock bag and freeze it.

I also freeze leftover sliced fruit such as pineapple, watermelon or even grapes – they taste delicious eaten frozen.

I like to make double batches of soup so that I can freeze any leftovers in portions.

I also freeze leftover sauces or meals that don't get finished, such as meatballs, bolognaise sauce or homemade baked beans. It's great to have a few homemade frozen meals ready to go when I feel like a night off cooking.

Leftover roast chicken is great for making fried rice the next day. And there are so many ways to cook a potato to add variety to a dinner. Making your own dressings, mayonnaise and dips is also cheaper than buying jars and at least I then know there are no preservatives and additives in it.

When I see leftover bread in the pantry, it's time to make breadcrumbs. I store them in a container in the freezer and they're delicious for making schnitzel, cauliflower with bread-crumbs and other dishes.

And I can never bring myself to buy a cake! They're so expensive and I can make my own in 10 minutes for hardly any cost at all.

Even these small ways of 'recycling' food can make a differ-ence to my weekly spending on food for our family.

CHAPTER 2:
Planning your meals

A LONG TIME AGO, before I had children, I used to look at meal planning and think it was just waayyyy too much work. But now I live by menu plans, and for an initial bit of effort they save me lots of time and energy during busy weeks, especially with hungry kids at night demanding to know what's for dinner. Meal planning can literally save you thousands of dollars per year, too, and is a totally integral part of *The $50 Weekly Shop*. Because if you have no plan, and you come home from a big day at work to cranky kids, it is very easy to fall into the trap of grabbing takeaway, or heating up processed foods, which we've seen are expensive!

Planning is crucial for shopping, too. Heading to the supermarket with the thought, 'I'll try to spend as little as possible' is doomed to failure. You've always got to have a plan because supermarkets are set up to make you spend as much as possible (that's why the milk is always in the furthest corner, so you have to walk past every other aisle to get to it).

So here we go!

When it comes to writing a menu plan, every family is different. Every diet is different and everyone has different likes and dislikes – which is why there is no 'one size fits all'. I've included several menu plans here as a guide, plus a couple of case studies, but really, it's up to you to come up with a menu plan (using the frugal recipes in this book) that suits your family's appetites, size, tastes and lifestyles.

For example, if your child does a lot of sport and you are travelling of an afternoon – think about the type of foods that are easy to transport and can be easily made ahead of time.

If you have five hungry boys, newborn babies or food intolerances, your diet will be different. But that doesn't mean you can't still cut costs.

So think about what's on your family calendar in the coming week. How many nights will you be out of the house with kids' sport or other extracurricular activities? How many people will be home to eat and how much food is required to get you through the next seven days? Plan ahead and save!

NICOLE'S STORY

I want to save money to be able to afford to pay for my kids' extracurricular activities and so that I can have a nice family holiday every year. I don't want to be rich, I just want to be comfortable, and living from pay to pay isn't any way to do that.

Yes, I've had to sacrifice things like takeaway and convenience foods. I no longer buy any expensive brands – I've gone back to cheaper or generic brands. I haven't bought clothing for myself for about three years, but will borrow from my friends instead for special occasions. There are just so many ways to save money from home.

In a typical week our family eats cheap meals that don't take a lot of time or energy to make. I do spend longer in the kitchen than I did before, but it is really paying off. I cook things like sausage casserole, stir-fries, and a lot more mince dishes as mince is so much cheaper than steak.

I now make a lot more the night before and take advantage of my leftovers. Hubby will take the leftovers for lunch the next day. I also no longer buy any of the pre-packaged snack food for the kids' lunches. Not only were they too expensive, but also full of sugar and this made the kids hyper and uncontrollable. I now do a bit of cooking on the weekend and freeze for the week. It has made a huge difference to our lifestyles.

Keep your kitchen clean and organised

'What does a clean kitchen have to do with meal planning?' I hear you ask. And the answer is, *a lot*! A messy, dirty or disorganised kitchen is not an appealing place to work in, and if you are serious about living frugally, you'll be doing a lot more cooking so you need to make your kitchen as inviting as possible.

Before you start, give your pantry, fridge and freezer a thorough going-over, clearing out expired foods, and cleaning all surfaces of dirt, spills and any vermin. Your freezer contents need to be labelled; your fridge shelves tidy and your pantry well organised so that you can see what ingredients you have. Storage containers for staples like flour, sugar, dry pasta and oats are a great idea and are inexpensive at variety stores. If you buy things in bulk, you can secure the opened packets and place them in large plastic tubs with well-fitting lids.

Make mealtimes a team effort

Lots of studies have found that families who sit down and eat dinner together are a lot happier than those who don't. It's also important for your family to pull their weight. Get the kids to help chop veggies or do other tasks like make the drinks, scrape the plates or stack/unload the dishwasher. If you cook, let hubby clean the kitchen. A family that works and plays together stays together!

Essential appliances and utensils

I know it sounds weird to have a section about this given that I'm all about saving money, but the appliances and utensils you have to hand can make or break a positive kitchen experience.

A decent-sized freezer: I have a large upright freezer (I used my Baby Bonus to buy it) and it is truly the best investment I've ever made!

A breadmaker: If you are dedicated to saving money, grab a bread-maker. Look for them in second-hand stores. (I've picked one up for $20!) They don't just make bread, you can use the mixers for making pizza dough, etc.

A slow cooker: These are brilliant. In fact, I have three of them because they are so handy. When you have very little money to spend, the slow cooker can be your best friend. It makes inexpensive pieces of meat into mouth-watering masterpieces. It can cook desserts, make snacks, drinks and even biscuits. If you are really busy during the day but want a delicious roast for dinner, you can't go past the slow cooker. And it isn't just chicken that can be cooked this way, lamb and beef are a winner too – although red meats do tend to 'shrink' a fair bit. Buy the biggest slow cooker you can afford so you can cook in bulk and freeze your leftovers. So easy, your pet cat could probably do it!

A food processor: Food processors save loads of time. I use them to grate my cheeses to freeze, do cake mixes and make pancakes. Of course, you can do all of these things by hand, too, so don't go out of your way to buy one if you don't have one already!

A hand-held blender (or stick blender): These are very handy for soups, smoothies, cakes, muffins and slices.

Sharp knives: Keep your knives in tip-top shape. Never put them in the dishwasher and sharpen them regularly. A blunt knife is a dangerous knife.

Chopping boards: Use the coloured plastic chopping boards that can be washed properly, and use different ones for meat, vegetables, fruit and bread, to reduce the risk of cross-contamination.

Frying pan: The bigger your family, the bigger your frying pan should be. And it doesn't need to be expensive. (I think I picked mine up from Ikea.)

Casserole dish: It's always good to have a couple of ceramic or pyrex casserole dishes of different sizes (medium and large). These are also easy to find second-hand, but don't forget that you can simply use a baking tray or even a cake tin. I quite often used my standard round cake tin for casseroles when I was poorer than I am now.

Pizza tray: Only grab one if you are an avid pizza lover! Otherwise, just use a baking tray or a biscuit tray.

Baking tins: A round cake tin and lamington tin (for slices) are essential. Muffin tins are also really handy. Pick them up when you see them on sale.

Make a list of your family's favourite dishes

To create a meal plan for your family, the first step is to identify the dishes that are currently on high rotation. These are meals that you make and serve regularly and that you know your family likes to eat. You should also include takeaway meals (or restaurant or pub meals if relevant) that they like to eat, as there are quite often versions you can easily make at home.

To use my own family as an example:

MY HIGH-ROTATION MEALS

BREAKFAST	LUNCH	DINNER	SNACKS
Porridge	Sandwiches	Lasagne	Fresh fruit (in season)
Peanut butter and banana on toast	Frittata made with leftovers	Sausage casserole	Homemade muffins
Cereal	Pita pizza	Chicken curry	
Muffins with baked beans	Baked beans on toast	Beef chow mein	Homemade slice
Scrambled eggs	Freezer meal	Spaghetti bolognaise	Hummus with rice crackers or veggie sticks
Breakfast burritos	Hamburgers	Tacos	
Pancakes		Pork chops and vegetables	
		Chicken pot pie	

Most of these meals we would have at least once a fortnight. If it makes it easier, do two weeks of meals that you make well and often.

Work out how to make these meals cheaper

The next step is to work out how to prepare these meals without wasting money. That means buying generic versions of the ingredients, buying ingredients in bulk and freezing some, bulking out the recipes with less expensive ingredients, and trying to include as many vegetarian versions of recipes that you can.

For the lasagne, I would buy my mince in bulk because I can also use it for the chow mien, the spaghetti bolognaise and the tacos. I'd brown all of the mince with onion and garlic and then either refrigerate or freeze what I don't use for the lasagne until I'm ready to use it for the chow mien or tacos.

I would bulk up my lasagne sauce with finely grated zucchini and carrot (the excellent hidden vegetable technique for fussy children). I would also add a tin of drained and washed lentils to the mix to make it go further – in fact I'd have enough bolognaise sauce left to make spaghetti bolognaise later in the week!

The sausage casserole is already pretty frugal, though for extra nutrition I'd serve it with some extra vegetables or even a salad.

Beef chow mein contains the mince I cooked earlier – plus I've added noodles (which are a staple and very cheap to buy) – and I would bulk it up with fresh or frozen vegetables. I'd make enough to have some for lunch the next day.

When making the spaghetti bolognaise – I'd cook extra spaghetti so that I could make some fritters for the boys for after school one night.

So going through each recipe and getting the most bang for your buck is truly the way to reduce your grocery costs – plus it usually ends up a lot healthier for you, too!

ANGELA B'S MEAL PLAN

Angela is a stay-at-home-mum from Leeming, Western Australia. She has three boys under six. One child is gluten-intolerant so Angela is buying a lot of premade meals to save time. All of the boys are very picky – they prefer sweet and unhealthy takeaway and processed foods. Unfortunately for Angela, this means she has to prepare two or three different meals at every sitting – she is exhausted and her food costs are going through the roof.

Here is what Angela's current week looks like (and every time you see something made with flour, know that Angela has to have gluten-free versions):

BREAKFAST	LUNCH	DINNER
Avocado on toast Porridge Scrambled eggs on toast	Fish fingers and chips	Steak, chips and eggs
Ham and cheese croissants	Mini meat pies Gluten free bread sandwiches	Nuggets and chips
Fruit salad with Greek yoghurt Boiled eggs with toast soldiers	Mini homemade pizzas Nachos	Macaroni cheese Avocado on toast with melted cheese

Pancakes with bacon and maple syrup	McDonald's (the kids 'demand' it)	Hot dogs with chips Tempura nuggets with potato gems
Omelettes (various flavours)	Sausages in bread with tomato sauce Ham and cheese toasted sandwiches	Roast lamb and vegetables
Nutella and strawberry topped cinnamon toast	Homemade hamburgers (chicken and beef)	Barbecue chicken (takeaway) with chips, gravy and coleslaw
Bacon and eggs	Lasagne	Pizza (takeaway)

Poor Angela. I can see why she is so stressed. Not only does she have to cater to different tastes, but having a child with gluten intolerance means she has to change many recipes. Plus, gluten-free products are very expensive! Here are my suggestions:

- **Cook only one evening meal each night:** It's not too hard to find simple, tasty meals that suit everyone.
- **Buy a breadmaker:** Gluten-free bread is ridiculously expensive (up to $7 a loaf). I would buy a large quantity of bread mix and use the breadmaker every night. If you think this is just adding to Angela's workload – it isn't. It literally takes 30 seconds to pop in the ingredients. If Angela puts the breadmaker on every night, every morning she will have freshly baked gluten-free bread that the whole family can enjoy.
- **Stop buying takeaway food:** Yes the kids will complain, but so what? Who's running this ship, anyway? Angela can cook up a few meals and freeze them for nights when she's just too exhausted to stand in front of the stove again. (I always keep at least six or seven servings of bolognaise sauce in my freezer. It can be served with pasta, in a pita wrap with cheese and lettuce, or on a baked potato with sour cream.

It can even be made into chilli con carne with a can of red kidney beans and a touch of chilli – so many options for so little cost!)

- **Buy only seasonal produce:** Yes, avocados are delicious. But only buy them when they are cheap (i.e. in season). Otherwise substitute them for something else. When it comes to breakfast, rice porridge is very cheap, very filling and all three kids can easily eat the same thing. Add some fresh seasonal fruit to the top. They will eat it if they are hungry!

- **Reserve cooked breakfasts and lunches for weekends if you are time poor:** Except for porridge – which can be cooked in the microwave in a few minutes – Angela should stick to easy meals that can be made without spending eons in the kitchen. A fully cooked breakfast and lunch is nice, but it is just creating a lot of work for a mum who is already tired and does need time to herself!

- **Don't be scared to repeat dishes:** The kids can eat the same breakfast or lunch more than once a week. And if they like it, even more than that. (My kids only eat honey and jam sandwiches – *every single day*. They refuse to eat anything else, so I sneak their vegetables in at dinner time instead. Some battles are just not worth fighting.)

Following my advice above, her weekly menu would look a bit like this (note that all of the recipes would use gluten-free flour, including the burritos):

BREAKFAST	LUNCH	DINNER
Rice porridge with fresh fruit	Mini sandwiches, fresh fruit and yoghurt	Gluten-free sausages with mashed potato and steamed vegetables
Toast with toppings of their choice	Ham and vegetable muffins, carrot sticks and hummus	Shepherd's pie

Breakfast burritos (can be heated in the microwave)	Chicken and salad wraps	Zucchini slice with steamed vegetables
Bacon and egg muffins (can be made in bulk with gluten-free flour, frozen and heated in the microwave)	Leftover zucchini slice, carrot sticks and cheese cubes	Tuna patties with mashed potato
French toast	Tuna patty sandwiches	Homemade baked potatoes with toppings of their choice
Baked beans on toast	Mini sandwiches	Crumbed sausages and vegetables
Fruit salad parfait	Home made pita pizza	Lentil lasagne

This menu is literally one third of the cost of Angela's first menu – plus it saves her a lot of time. Many of the recipes can be cooked in bulk and frozen for another day, giving Angela more time to herself.

Be flexible

The biggest mistake people make with meal planning is to be too rigid. For example, 'On Mondays we will have lasagne, on Tuesdays we will have fish and homemade chips . . .' etc. That is *way* too hard. Your meal plan will vary depending on the foods you need to use up before they go 'off'. It also depends on what the weather is like. Cold weather means more soups, casseroles, roasts and root vegetables; while summer is all about salads and barbecues and fresh fruit. Also, life tends not to go according to plan, so on those nights you're rushed off your feet you'll need to grab something out of the freezer to reheat. Then on those rare, lazy days where you have more time, you can make something special. It's all about balance and what works for your family.

Rather than locking in specific recipes for particular nights, why not use broad categories such as cuisines or styles of preparation. For example:

MONDAY	Italian (pizza or pasta)
TUESDAY	Soup, herb bread and salad
WEDNESDAY	Mexican (tacos or burritos)
THURSDAY	Curry night
FRIDAY	Make your own (leftovers, whatever is in the fridge – mainly for families with older children)
SATURDAY	Baked potatoes (with a variety of toppings)
SUNDAY	Slow-cooked casserole

Try new things

To make your meal plans work, you need to feed your family meals that they like to eat (hence the initial brainstorm of their favourite foods!). But there are many more cheap and easy meals that your family may not have tried. So perhaps once a fortnight, introduce a new dish. Just one meal – there's no point making a huge batch only to find out that your family won't eat it. So trawl websites, food forums and magazines (and the recipes in this book of course) to see what may appeal to your family.

One thing my dad used to do was to go through all Mum's cookbooks and tick the recipes that he'd like to try one day. Dad was a brilliant cook – and we always got to try something a little different. So don't be scared to get out of your comfort zone once in a while and just give something a go! Might be the best meal you've ever eaten!

Here are some websites that might give you some great ideas for new recipes:

- stayathomemum.com.au
- foodgawker.com
- allrecipes.com.au
- au.pinterest.com
- instagram.com

Always keep a shopping list

Check your meal plan for the upcoming week and write down all of the ingredients you will need to buy, excluding the items you already have in the pantry, fridge or freezer. (And if you do notice that you have foods that are about to go 'off' or reach their 'best before date', remember that you need to use those foods up!)

Keep your shopping list somewhere where you will see it all the time. I keep mine on a spreadsheet open on my computer (because I'm on the computer all day) – but I used to keep it on my fridge door. (I attached some old magnets to the back so it would stay there!) You can also keep it in your phone if you prefer; that way you will be less likely to leave it at home!

I also have a 'master list' for shopping. This is a template I use when I have absolutely nothing in the house and don't need to just 'top up' for the week. The master template contains many of the pantry staples that will make multiple meals. I've included that template here for you to look at. You don't need to have all of these in your cupboard – only those that you will use again and again.

FRUIT & VEGGIES	DAIRY	TINS & JARS	FROZEN	STAPLES	CEREALS	BAKING	DELI	MEATS	OTHER	SCHOOL LUNCHES	DRINKS

LYDIA W'S MEAL PLAN

Lydia is from Gympie, Queensland, and is a busy mum with two kids at high school. Her husband commutes to another town for work, and Lydia also works thirty hours a week, so she is always super busy managing the household on her own. Her son, Eligh, is a soccer champion in the making. He trains four nights a week and Lydia has to travel up to an hour every evening (sometimes straight from school with both her son and daughter in the car) to get him to training. They often don't get home until nine or 10 at night.

Nutrition is hugely important for Lydia and her family. She is a wonderful cook and her kids love foods like salmon and sushi – which can get quite expensive. Her son needs lots of protein for training and loves eggs. She is very busy and needs quick nutritious, transportable meals as takeaway is an expensive and unhealthy option. Luckily for Lydia, she has a couple of chooks in the backyard! At the moment, Lydia's average five-day meal plan looks like this:

BREAKFAST	LUNCH	DINNER
Poached eggs on toast	Salmon sushi rolls with a salad and bread roll	Sizzler
Salmon and chive omelettes	Ham and salad rolls	Lamb shanks with roast vegetables
Porridge with fresh fruit and yoghurt	Chicken sausage rolls and crunchy noodle salad	Takeaway vegetable tempura
Poached eggs on toast	School tuckshop	Takeaway burgers
Bacon and eggs	Chicken sushi rolls	Mixed grill with mashed potato

Her breakfasts are already good value seeing she doesn't need to spend money on eggs. Plus they are healthy and filling and a great start for the day.

For lunches, I would replace the salmon with tuna or chicken, which are cheaper options but still contain a lot of protein. I'd maybe even add a boiled egg or two to their lunchboxes.

Dinner is something she will need to prepare in advance and be able to 'travel' with. I would encourage Lydia to set up her slow cooker before work, and have her main meals all cooked for when she gets home. The meals can then be transferred to a thermos to keep them warm until dinner time – and they can even be eaten in the car (depending on how far she has to travel). This would save her from having to buy expensive takeaway food three or four nights a week, and would be a much healthier option.

A more frugal weekday plan for Lydia could go something like this:

BREAKFAST	LUNCH	DINNER
Poached eggs on toast	Vegetable sushi rolls	Pumpkin soup (served in a thermos) with wholemeal bread rolls
Salmon and chive omelettes	Greek salad with bread rolls	Stir-fry with chicken or fish, vegetables and rice
Porridge with fresh fruit and yoghurt	Leftover stir-fry and rice	Slow-cooker pea and ham soup (served in a thermos) with toasted cheesies
Poached eggs on toast	Hummus and salad wraps	Slow-cooker lasagne
Bacon and eggs	Tuna sushi rolls	Leftover lasagne

CHAPTER 3:
Shopping for ingredients

WHEN IT COMES TO actually doing your grocery shopping, the most important (and obvious) tip is to remember to take your list. If you are notorious for forgetting it, download a shopping list app and keep it on your phone. Of course, having a list doesn't guarantee you're going to stick to it – supermarkets can be seductive places – so here are the best ways I know to help you avoid impulse buys:

- Pay cash instead of using a card. (Use the internet to work out how much your items will cost before you go, it forces you to keep to your budget.)
- Take a calculator (or use your phone) and add up what you are spending as you go.
- Never shop when you are hungry. (I know you've heard it before – but it makes a *huge* difference.)
- Try not to shop with young children – it's distracting for you and stressful for everyone (especially if they're hassling you nonstop to buy toys or sweets and you're not giving in!). If shopping with preschoolers is unavoidable, give them a special 'job' to do (putting stuff in the trolley), or put them in the trolley with a colouring book!

- Bring your own bottle of water and sip it to get you past the chocolate, soft drink and snack aisles.
- Avoid shopping at peak times (Saturday mornings and 3–5 p.m. weekdays).
- If you keep to your budget, give yourself a small, inexpensive treat as a reward (or just put a couple of dollars in a piggy bank to save up for something just for you).
- Every day remind yourself of the reason you are budgeting, perhaps by having a note or a photo of your goal on the fridge.

The only time you should stray from your list is when you encounter an unexpected sale on staple items that you just can't go past. In such cases, if it's a tremendous deal and you can afford to do so, buy up big. It might go over your budget now, but in the long run it will save you money.

Comparing prices

In the past, unless you were a maths whiz it was hard to work out which products were the best value for money. Fortunately, since 2009 it's been compulsory for every supermarket to provide a unit price for every item so that shoppers can quickly compare costs. Unit pricing breaks the cost of a product into a unit of weight, volume or number. For example, chocolate will have a unit price per 100 g, milk a unit price per litre and a bulk pack of breakfast bars or drinks might list an 'each' price.

In most cases, the larger the size or amount, the smaller the unit price. For example, the unit price of a 1-litre bottle of soft drink might be $1.20 per litre, yet for a 2-litre bottle it might be $0.90 per litre. However, when buying in bulk, don't always assume that you are getting a good deal. Sometimes it is actually cheaper to buy multiples of the smaller packs. So always check the unit price before you purchase.

Catalogues and loyalty cards

I'm a firm believer in going through all of the supermarket catalogues to see what specials are on. (I have to do it online as I live in the country.) But a shop would have to offer at least three fantastic deals to make it worth my while to make a special trip there – otherwise I'm just wasting money on fuel. The specials also have to be on great staples that I know I will use and that won't go stale or off.

Personally, I love Aldi and I try to make a trip to Costco at least once a month. And even though Woolworths, Coles and IGA are reputedly more expensive than the others, they still have to offer decent specials to get people through the door.

It's also a great idea to join any loyalty programs your supermarket may have, every cent saved is a cent earned! I have stacks of loyalty cards, and to stop my purse from exploding, I downloaded an app called 'Stocard', but there are many similar apps available. For each loyalty card you get, you simply enter its details and then you can throw it away. Every time you need to swipe your loyalty card, just open the app and it's all in there!

Comparing quality

Unit pricing might be great for working out which items are cheaper, but it can't help you decide on quality. When you are concerned about finding products without gluten, or ones that are low in sugar or high in fibre, you are going to have to read the labels. And in Australia, all nutrition labels have to include information about any allergens (milk, eggs, nuts, seeds, gluten) that the item may contain. In addition, all packaged foods (except freshly baked goods) must have a table showing the proportions of fat, salt and sugar per 100 g. This makes it easy to work out which foods are healthier for you.

Which supermarket is the cheapest?

This is a very good question, and not an easy one to answer. I can honestly say that although I do most of my shopping at Aldi, I do shop around for specials elsewhere depending on what they have on sale and whether it is worth my while to make the trip in the car to buy it.

To prove that there is no 'cheapest supermarket' I actually put all the supermarkets to the test in Adelaide last year. Having the exact same shopping list – and buying the exact same brands – I was surprised to find that there isn't one particular supermarket that is cheaper all round. Each had strengths and weaknesses in terms of value items. So the saying to 'shop around' is very true.

Going online to check out the specials is a great way to know which supermarket to visit. A lot of supermarkets have huge specials that they make absolutely no money on to 'get you in the door' – so get in the door, but only buy that special! Don't get sucked in by all the other merchandise!

If you are looking for quality over quantity, small butcher and fruit and vegetable chains did substantially better than the name brand supermarkets when I was comparing them. Plus, you can always haggle, and if you are a regular customer you're more likely to not only get better produce, but also a better deal. Small outlets also need to turn over their stock a lot faster than the larger supermarkets – so you can, say, buy a tray of apples that are slightly bruised for as low as a quarter of the original price. Hunt around for these types of specials – they are what will save you money in the long run.

WHERE TO FIND THE CHEAPEST ITEMS IN A SUPERMARKET

Supermarkets are very careful about where they put produce – they obviously want us to spend as much money as possible and they have canny ways of tricking unwary customers. First of all, never shop at eye level – that's where the supermarket promotes the product with the highest profit share. Brands pay a premium to have their products at eye-level for people who don't care too much about what they're buying and just want to grab it and go.

But frugal shoppers are smarter than that! The best place to look first is right down the bottom at floor level. Then look up at the top shelf. But the truly best place of all to find the cheapest items is at the ends of the aisles. This is where the supermarket places bulk items that they want to get rid of quickly – and they will sell them at close to cost price. Take advantage of this – especially with staple items.

Most supermarkets also have a clearance section, or a section with items close to their best-before date. It is often a trolley or stand at the back of the store, or a low shelf in the refrigerated section. Either way, you will find the clearance section to be a messy, uncoordinated pile. And this discourages most shoppers – but don't let it discourage you. If you are patient enough to weed through this section for items on your list, you may just find that special something at a terrific price and save even more dollars.

If you are particularly adventurous, some supermarkets will sell tins of food that have lost their labels. Sure, you don't know what is in there, but you can guarantee it will be some kind of food and that it will be super cheap!

SOME THINGS ARE WORTH PAYING FOR

I realise that we are all about low-cost shopping and frugality here, but we are also about doing the right thing, and there are some foods that I buy that may not necessarily be the cheapest at the time.

Wherever possible, I buy locally grown or produced food including fruit, vegetables, milk, cheese, honey, coffee, wine, etc. If you can't afford to buy local stuff, at least make sure it is grown or produced somewhere in Australia. (When I'm shopping at Aldi, I make sure I buy foods that are made here.) I value our farmers and always buy my local brand of milk. (The more money we put into the supply chain, the greater the chance that milk processors can pay more to the farmers.) Personally, I think it's outrageous that milk is cheaper than bottled water – it is expensive and time-consuming to produce, and we should pay our farmers properly for it.

Where to buy staples in bulk

Of course, the supermarket isn't always the cheapest place to buy, especially if you are able to buy in bulk. There are loads of other places you can try to get more bang for your buck. (I love Costco!)

ONLINE STORES

There are loads of online stores that now sell bulk food items at discounted prices. Not just food either – cleaning supplies, nappies, toilet paper – anything for the household at a budget price. Try places like Grocery Run, Ozsale or even Groupon.

LOCAL MARKETS AT CLOSING TIME

This is a great time to buy fruit and vegetables.

LOCAL FARMERS

Countryside road stalls are a great place to look for seasonal produce. Look at finding a farm that sells whole beasts. Sometimes you can 'lay by' a cow and they will cut it up for you. This can work out as cheap as $7 a kilo.

LOCAL BUTCHERS

Many butchers now have 'bulk freezer packs' that contain roasts, sausages, rissoles, etc. – all of which are highly discounted compared to individual purchase prices.

ASIAN GROCERS

Asian food stores are a fantastic place to get many foods cheaply, including lots of delicious staples, herbs, spices and sauces. Some sell 20 kg bags of rice – of course you'd need to have somewhere to store them!

FLOUR MILLS

Bakery distributors are the perfect place to pick up bulk flours (especially if you require gluten free or specialty flours). I've listed a few of the main bakery distributors here – you can go online and order whatever you like. The main disadvantage is postage.

- fourleafmilling.com.au
- wholegrain.com.au
- laucke.com.au

CHEAP VARIETY STORES

You would probably think that your nearest $2 shop would be the last place to find cheap food items, but it is worth having a look. Sometimes you'll find spaghetti sauces, nuts and dried fruits, canned tuna or salmon, rice, olives, soups and cereals. The cheap stores are also a good place to pick up coffee and tea bags and discounted cleaning products.

CHAPTER 4:
Avoiding waste

AUSTRALIANS WASTE ABOUT 25 per cent of the food they buy, either because it goes bad before they cook it or they just throw away the leftovers. That works out to about $1000 per year worth of food for each household. You may as well get $1000 out of the bank and just cut it up! Don't do it any more – make use of every single item of food you purchase. If you start thinking of the dollar value you are losing when you throw food away, it may make you think twice about that wastage.

How to store stuff so it lasts longer

More than once I've found fruit and vegetables at the bottom of my vegetable crisper that have created a pool of stinky brown liquid. (By the way, if this happens to you, dig that liquid straight into your garden for instant fertiliser!) The problem with my crisper is that I can't actually *see* what's in there, so I forget about it. Fortunately, I've found a great way to store fruit and veg so that they're not only more visible, but also last as long as possible (before liquefaction).

Avocados: Keep avocados in a paper bag if you want to stop them from ripening too fast. Actually, this is good for any fruit. Also, if you only use half the avocado, cut it lengthways so you can keep the stone in place. Then brush the exposed flesh with a little lemon juice to prevent oxidation and seal tightly with plastic wrap.

Bananas: Buy bananas in small quantities as they tend to go black very easily. Never store bananas in the fridge – they go black very quickly and lose all their delicious flavour. Keep them in your fruit bowl (which should always be on the bench where you do your cooking so you don't forget to use your fruit). To keep bananas for longer, wrap the end of the bunch with plastic wrap. It blocks the release of ethylene from the stem that makes the bananas ripen quickly. If you have missed your 'window' and your bananas are overripe, pop them out of their skins and into a zip-lock bag and straight into the freezer. They are wonderful for smoothies, cakes and best of all, **Banana Ice Cream**. (Just place a couple of frozen bananas in a food processor and process until smooth – for **Banana and Chocolate Ice Cream**, add half a cup of Nutella.)

Bread: Keep your bread fresher for longer by putting a celery stick in the bag. The bread slowly absorbs moisture from the celery, keeping the bread soft. The taste of celery is so mild it doesn't affect the taste of the bread. If you live in a warmer part of the country, keep your sliced bread in the freezer and take out pieces as required.

Brown sugar: To stop your brown sugar going hard, keep a few marshmallows in the container. It will always be soft.

Cakes: To keep cut cakes fresh, secure a slice of bread to the cut side with some toothpicks.

Celery: Even if you don't like the taste of raw celery, the flavour is wonderful in soups and casseroles. You can buy celery in whole or half bunches or just a few stalks at once. Celery can't be used raw once frozen (it turns mushy and gross), but you can freeze sliced celery and use it to make soup. To make celery last longer, give it a really good wash (you would be surprised how much dirt can get in between the stalks) and wrap the whole lot in aluminium foil. It will then last up to six weeks instead of wilting after just a few days.

Cheese: If you buy tasty cheddar in bulk, you risk it going mouldy or hard. I buy 1 kg blocks on sale, grate the lot in my food processor, and freeze it in small zip-lock bags. Grated cheese freezes and thaws very well.

Cottage cheese: To make cottage cheese last longer, all you need to do is to turn the container upside down, which will create a vacuum so air can't get in. This prevents bacteria from growing.

Flour: When you get your flour home, sift it well into a zip-lock bag and seal, removing as much as air as possible. Store it in the freezer to keep it fresh and to prevent it being contaminated by moths and weevils.

Ginger: There is nothing quite like the taste of fresh ginger. However, it is tremendously expensive, so don't waste what you don't use. Peel it and freeze in a zip-lock bag, ready to grate whenever you need that lovely fresh ginger taste.

Mushrooms: Never wash mushrooms, as they absorb water and tend to go slimy. If they are dirty, just get a damp (not wet) cloth and give them a rub. Store them in the fridge in a paper bag but use them as quickly as you can. They will only last in the fridge for about four days before starting to wrinkle, though even when they are a little wrinkled, you can still finely chop them and add them to rissoles or stews.

Onions: Like spuds, onions need to be kept in a dark place with good air circulation – so no plastic bags. Keep onions and potatoes in separate baskets as they tend to cause each other to rot if they are placed together. Better still, why not chop up your onions and freeze them? I really don't like chopping onions, so I put on my swimming goggles (or put the onions in the fridge overnight first) and dice the whole lot! Then I place the equivalent of about half an onion in a small freezer bag, pushing out as much air as I can. It freezes beautifully – and every time I need onion in a recipe I have a little bag in the freezer ready to go.

Potatoes: These need to be taken out of their plastic bags as soon as you get home from the shops. (Better still, don't use plastic and just put all of your veggies in a reusable cloth bag.) When you get your spuds home, store them in a dark place that allows for good air circulation. I use a simple basket and place it in the bottom of the pantry.

Pumpkin: Pumpkin stores well if you cut it in half, remove all of the seeds and chop it into large chunks. (Leave the skin on until you're ready to cook it.) Pop the chunks into a zip-lock bag, get as much air out as possible and keep in the crisper until needed. It will stay fresh for 10 days. If you are roasting pumpkin, leave the skin on. Even if you don't like the skin, it bakes better and makes the pumpkin tastier. You can always peel it off after cooking, although when baked, the skin is quite tasty.

Rice, cooked: This one is terrific. Rice is notorious for giving people food poisoning. It can't be cooked and left in the fridge for any more than two days as it goes bad so quickly. But if you have leftover rice, you can either make a delicious rice pudding, or freeze it for later. Place a cup at a time in a medium zip-lock bag (jiggle it around a bit to separate the grains into an even layer), seal and freeze. When you need fresh rice, remove it from the zip-lock, place in a microwave container with a splash of stock or water and reheat until ready!

Stock: Whether you make your own or buy premade cartons, stock is a great staple item. However, if you open the carton of the premade version and don't use the whole lot, freeze it – otherwise it will just die at the back of your fridge somewhere and be thrown out. To freeze stock, pour it into ice cube trays then transfer the frozen cubes into a zip-lock bag. Stock will freeze well for up to six months.

Tomatoes: The best tomatoes in the world are those grown in your own backyard and picked fresh. If this isn't possible, buy them from a local grocer or market where, hopefully, they've been grown with just as much love. For many years I hated tomatoes because they had a bland, almost chalky taste – then I tried a home-grown version! Don't place tomatoes in the fridge – store them in your fruit basket in full view. If they are not quite ripe, keep them on a windowsill where they will get a bit of sunlight.

DEFROSTING AND THAWING

The best way to defrost frozen foods is to take them out of the freezer and leave them in the fridge overnight. This especially applies to frozen meats. I'm not a big fan of defrosting meat in the microwave because it can sometimes 'cook' part of your food, making it hard to cook evenly (and microwaves are expensive to run). If you forget to take your meat out of the freezer, remove it from any packaging and place it in a sealed zip-lock bag (make sure it has no holes). Fill your sink with hot tap water (don't use boiling water or you will 'cook' the meat) and pop the bag into the water. It should defrost in less than 10 minutes.

Money-saving tips from the Depression era

During the Great Depression of the 1930s, people wasted *nothing*. Every scrap of everything was used – often more than once. The mantra of the Depression era was 'Use it up, wear it out, make it do, or do without.' The tips on the next page go beyond the wastage of food, but I wanted to put them in here because they are such an amazing contrast to the entitled, wasteful, throwaway society we live in today.

Make it stretch: Get another week out of your bottle of sauce or jar of mayo by adding a few drops of water, giving it a shake and keeping it upside down! Then reuse the container for next week's homemade sauce.

Reuse and recycle: Think twice before throwing anything out. I keep all of the jars that I'm not using to give to a friend of mine who likes to make jam, and I get a few jars of goodies in return. I even keep butter containers – they're great to use for fruit for the kids' school lunches and it doesn't matter so much if they don't make it home.

Refurbish or buy second-hand: Rather than buying a new lounge suite or dining room table, look at buying a second-hand one in good nick. See if someone is giving one away that you can do up yourself, or look at the one you currently have and see if it will do for a bit longer or can be sanded back, painted or made to look new again.

Grow your own food: You don't need much room to grow a few herbs or some lettuce, tomatoes or zucchini, and it is a truly rewarding experience. Plus, supermarket tomatoes always taste terrible unless you can afford the expensive truss ones. There is nothing like home-grown goodness! See page 75 for information on growing your own veggies.

Save up for things: These days, people seem to have lost the ability to wait. We expect to press a button and get everything we want instantly. As a kid I couldn't just go and buy whatever I wanted – my parents gave us pocket money and we had to work towards it. Do that now and save up for something rather than putting it on the credit card – it will certainly make you appreciate it more.

Make it at home: Instead of going out for burgers or pizza, make them at home. Cook more and go out less. Spend more time with your family and less time shopping – it's not only cheaper, but benefits how close you are as a family. Think about making your own ice cream, bread and relish. Get the kids involved in baking muffins, biscuits and slices.

Eat less: Compared to earlier generations, we are eating way too much and moving way too little. Our portion sizes are *huge*, which is one reason why we are an obese nation. We're also eating way too much sugar. Living frugally is also about managing portion sizes – you can't help but lose weight as a result. It is a win–win situation.

Separate your needs and wants: You might *want* the latest iPhone – but do you really need it? You might want Netflix, but you don't need it. Think about how you can make do with what you have. Eating out or getting takeaway is a prime example. For a single night's $30 takeaway chicken meal, you could buy enough groceries to feed your family for at least three days – probably more! Think before getting that card out of your purse.

Find things to do that are free: Not everything worth doing costs money! In fact, sometimes the opposite is true. Check out your local library – you'll be amazed at what you can borrow (movies, books, music, games). Or simply Google 'free entertainment' in your area. Go to a local market or simply get the kids outside playing a game of cricket. There really isn't any need to spend a fortune on entertainment when you can save a heap and still have a great time – at home!

Encourage everyone to contribute: If you are living as frugally as possible and still can't manage to make ends meet, it might be time to find ways to bring more money into your household. Can you or your partner do some additional hours? There are always options for making more money – packing shelves, delivering pamphlets, writing articles, cleaning. Are your kids old enough to do some babysitting or odd jobs around the neighbourhood? And if your kids are all grown up but still live at home, charge them rent or board.

Creative uses for leftovers

Perhaps the most obvious way to save money on food is to use up every ingredient you buy and everything you cook. This means that if there's anything left in the pan (or even on someone's plate!), it should be sealed in a container and used to create another meal. If it hasn't already been thawed once, it can be frozen for a later use. Here are some of the best tips I've learned:

COOKED MEAT

Apart from the obvious sandwiches and wraps, there are endless ways to use leftover meat:

- Make fritters (page 191).
- Add to a vegetable stir-fry.
- Toss it through a salad or some cooked pasta with mayo, pesto or sweet chilli sauce.
- Add it to The 'Baked Potato' Buffet (page 180).
- Use it for 'What Ya Got' Casserole (page 181).

BONES AND CARCASSES

These are gold for making stock (page 102). Keep them in the freezer until you need them. If I ever buy a cooked chook, once I've used up the meat, I use the carcass to make stock!

BREAD

Stale bread can be used in stacks of ways:

- Blitz it in a food processor to make breadcrumbs (dry in the oven first if you prefer).
- Make Slow-cooker Bread and Butter Pudding (page 310).
- Make croutons by cutting off the crusts, cutting into small squares, spraying with a little canola oil and frying or baking in the oven for a few minutes (see Easy Garlic Croutons recipe, page 90).

- Make it into **Garlic Bread.** (Spread with a mixture of crushed garlic and butter, wrap in foil and pop in a moderate oven for 10 minutes, then open the foil and cook for a few more minutes to crisp up.)

If your kids like you to cut the crusts off their sandwiches, don't throw the crusts away – keep them in a sealed bag in the freezer. And they are a great way to keep stuffing inside a chicken while it's roasting. Just insert the stuffing, then wedge in the crust. Plus it is delicious once it has absorbed all the flavours of the roast chicken and stuffing while baking!

CEREAL

Stale cereal happens in any household. Maybe the kids decided that they didn't like that kind of cereal any more; maybe there wasn't enough cereal for a full bowl, or maybe they just don't like the dregs at the bottom. As long as your cereal isn't rancid or moth-ridden, here are some ingenious ways to use it up:

- **Crumbs:** Crush the cereal until it resembles breadcrumbs then use it to coat chicken pieces or to make patties.
- **Muffin mix:** Loosely crush the cereal and add it to any muffin recipe, or better still, mix it with a little sugar and melted butter and pop it on top of your muffins to make a crumble!
- **Flour substitute:** High fibre cereal can be crushed to create a 'flour' and used as substitute for a quarter of the regular white flour in most recipes.
- **Dessert topper:** Mix the cereal with a little butter and brown sugar, bake for a few minutes in the oven, and have as a topper over any dessert. It is lovely on ice cream or sprinkled over iced chocolate.
- **Bake and reuse:** Stale cereal can be 'bought back to life' by placing it in the oven for a couple of minutes at low heat to re-crisp. Then serve with milk as normal.

- **Snack bars:** Use them to make Leftover Cereal Bars (page 300) – much better than the sugary muesli bars available at the supermarket.
- **Bird food:** Okay, so if it is really inedible (and doesn't contain too much sugar), it makes for good bird food!

VEGGIES

- If you have an abundance of spring onions (this can happen if you grow them yourself!), chop them all up and freeze them in an empty plastic bottle. Then you can just 'pour out' what you need and put the bottle back in the freezer.
- Got some carrot skins, broccoli stalks or wilted lettuce leaves? Don't throw them out – freeze them until you are ready to make stock. Or find someone who has chickens or pigs – they will be very grateful and might give you a few eggs or some bacon here and there. All better options than landfill.
- Any grated veggies or stalks that are still edible but not worth putting back in the fridge can be popped into a bolognaise sauce or frozen in a zip-lock bag and added to your next soup.
- I love to make loads of extra baked vegetables (especially potato, sweet potato and pumpkin). They are delicious added to a salad of leafy greens, beetroot and feta cheese (very schmancy!)
- Leftover mashed potato can be made into croquettes (page 142) or potato cakes (page 144) – the kids just love these!
- Always wash your potatoes before peeling. (By the way, unwashed potatoes are always cheaper to buy, last longer and are more delicious!) To make **Crispy Potato Skins**, you'll need to have peels that are fairly thick. Place the peels on a baking tray, salt well and bake at 200°C until crispy! They are so yummy – I love them dipped in a little mayo or pesto.

FRUIT

If you're constantly throwing out fruit because it turns into a puddle, then these tips are for you!

- Apples and pears can be grated and added to any cake recipe to make it super moist.
- Apples can also be peeled and cooked into apple puree – which is a great substitute for sugar in sweet recipes.
- Citrus fruit can be juiced and zested.
- Bananas can be frozen for smoothies, ice cream or banana cake.
- Make a **Fruit Crumble**. Just peel and dice any sad looking fruit, add a little coconut and brown sugar, top with rolled oats and bake until golden.

OTHER KITCHEN SCRAPS

Don't throw away used coffee grounds, egg shells and tea bags – these can all be used as a great fertiliser for the garden (discard the bag from the teabag first).

Getting the most out of your ingredients

Citrus fruit: To get more juice out of a lemon, lime or orange, put it in the microwave for about 10 seconds, then roll it back and forth on the bench a few times, pressing gently. You will get twice as much juice out of it!

Wine: Rather than watering down precious wine with ice cubes, use frozen grapes. They are not only delicious, but also won't melt and ruin your wine!

Honey: When a recipe requires, say, a tablespoon or cup of honey, molasses or other syrup, spray the spoon or cup with a little canola oil before you pour the syrup or honey in. When you add it to your recipe, it will just 'fall out' and you won't waste a drop!

Coconut milk: If your recipe calls for coconut milk, buy one tin of coconut cream, mix with water and you will get the equivalent of two cans of coconut milk for the same price!

Yoghurt: Rather than buying flavoured yoghurt, which is full of sugar, buy plain Greek-style yoghurt so that you can use it for cooking as well as for desserts (just add fresh fruit!) Also, never buy individual yoghurts for school lunches (unless they are on special!). Buy a bulk sized version and transfer the yoghurt into small reusable containers (they'll need very secure lids). This will save you up to $1 per school lunch, per child!

'Making do'

Knowing how to substitute ingredients in your cooking is another brilliant way to avoid waste and therefore save money (and time). It's great to know what to use if you run out of a particular ingredient, and you'll be surprised at just how many foods can be substituted – and for what.

Baking powder: Baking powder is a rising agent for cakes and biscuits. To make your own baking powder, mix together one part bicarbonate of soda, with two parts cream of tartar.

Breadcrumbs: Make your own using fresh crusts or day-old bread. Simply tear it up and pulse in a food processor until it reaches the desired texture. Or, if you have no bread to use, here are some other options:
- Oat bran.
- Rolled oats, puffed rice or other plain cereal (crushed or processed to crumbs in a food processor).
- Crushed crackers.
- Crushed potato chips.
- Desiccated coconut.
- Finely crushed nuts.

Butter: Well, the most obvious substitute is margarine, but a lot of people don't like the fact that margarine is so heavily processed, plus it doesn't taste as good. You can sometimes use vegetable or nut oils, but be aware that their flavour can affect what you are cooking, so judge accordingly. If it's just for toast in the morning, consider using cottage cheese or just leave it out and enjoy the flavour of the topping! Or if you have some cream, make your own butter (page 98).

Other substitutes for fats in cooking include:

- Apple puree (for cakes and muffins)
- Avocados (for savoury dishes)
- Mashed bananas (for sweet dishes)
- Prunes (combine ¾ cup prunes with ¼ cup boiling water and puree – great in sweet dishes)
- Chia seeds (combine 1 tablespoon of chia seeds with 180 ml of hot water – allow to sit for 15 minutes or until it forms a jelly).

Buttermilk: Buttermilk is available in the dairy section of your super-market but as it expires quickly, it's not something most people have on hand (although it does freeze well so don't let it go to waste if you do have it!). To make your own substitute at home, take 1 cup of ordi-nary milk, add 2 teaspoons of lemon juice or vinegar and let it stand in a warm place for five minutes. If you're out of milk, too, just use the same quantity of sour cream or natural yoghurt.

Cocoa powder: If you need a substitute for cocoa powder, use 25 g of chocolate bits for every tablespoon of cocoa powder, but make sure you reduce the fats in the recipe by 1 tablespoon. You may also use Dutch-processed cocoa plus ⅛ teaspoon of either lemon juice, white vinegar or cream of tartar.

Condensed milk: Condensed milk can be made at home. Combine 1 cup of powdered milk with ¾ cup white sugar and ½ cup warm water. Mix until well combined and store in the fridge. Makes the equivalent of one standard can of milk. (I have another recipe for sweetened condensed milk on page 99.)

Cream: Cream can be replaced with evaporated milk, thickened with cornflour if required. Another replacement is a 3:1 ratio of full-cream milk and butter. Depending on the recipe, other cream replacements could be:

- sour cream
- Greek yoghurt
- cream cheese.

Cream of tartar: Small amounts of cream of tartar (less than ½ teaspoon) can be substituted with the same quantity of lemon juice or white vinegar.

Eggs: Egg substitutes depend on what you are cooking. For sweet recipes, 1 tablespoon of custard powder per egg works a treat. For a dairy-free version, try 1 small mashed banana or ½ cup apple sauce (apple puree is also a great sugar replacement!). For savoury dishes, try 2 tablespoons of cornflour per egg. Chia seeds also work well as an egg replacement for either sweet or savoury dishes. Combine 1 table-spoon of chia seeds with 1 cup of water and let it sit for 15 minutes. This makes a perfect 1:1 egg ratio for baking.

Honey: Depending on the recipe, golden syrup, treacle or molasses make good substitutes for honey.

Lemon juice: If you need a substitute for the citrus flavour, try orange or lime juice. If you need its acidic qualities for dressings or other uses, use white vinegar.

Maple syrup: To replace 1 cup of maple syrup, use ½ cup golden syrup and simply increase the liquid in the recipe by ¼ cup. Another option is to combine ¾ cup corn syrup, ¼ cup of butter and an optional ½ teaspoon of maple extract. Or just use honey.

Milk: Milk has many replacement options:
- 1:1 mix of evaporated milk and water.
- 12:1 mix of water and melted butter (for baking cakes, muffins etc) i.e. 1 cup water and 1½ tablespoons melted butter .
- 1:1 mix of cream and water.
- 1:1 mix of sour cream and water, plus 25:1 mix of sugar (e.g. ½ cup sour cream, ½ cup water, ½ teaspoon sugar).

Salt: The best replacement for 1 teaspoon of salt is a stock cube.

Self-raising flour: To make your own self-raising flour, add 2 teaspoons of baking powder to 1 cup of plain flour. If you have no baking powder, see page 62!

Sugar: These days, many people are cutting down on sugar, and for good reason. (The World Health Organization reckons that no more than 10 per cent of our calories should come from added sugar, and this includes the sugar in soft drinks, confectionary, ice cream, processed foods, and even fruit juice.) Some alternatives to sugar include honey, apple puree, stevia and erythritol (Natvia).

Wine: White wine can be substituted with chicken or vegetable stock and red wine with beef stock.

Yoghurt: If you do not have any yoghurt to hand, you can opt to use sour cream instead. Buttermilk is also a great substitute, but if you can't find it, check out how to make a substitute on page 63!

How to add flavour to 'boring' food

Here are some interesting ways to pack a flavour punch to foods you may be finding a bit bland:

- Add a pinch of lemon, lime or orange zest to cereal, rice, cooked meat or even a pasta dish.
- Honey is lovely on top of porridge, on toast or in tea instead of sugar.
- Add a teaspoon of butter to cooked porridge, rice, vegetables – anything, really. Butter makes everything better – just ask the French!
- Sprinkle cinnamon or nutmeg over porridge, pumpkin soup, hot-buttered toast, rice pudding or cooked apple for a warm, spicy touch.
- Don't forget good old salt and pepper! A well seasoned dish is a tasty dish. Freshly cracked pepper is always a winner, and whole peppercorns are not expensive to buy.
- Finely sliced red onion (Spanish onion) is delicious in salads and sandwiches – a real burst of flavour.
- Grow some basil and parsley in your back yard. They are not only easy to grow (see chapter 5) but also delicious washed, chopped and stirred through pretty much any savoury dish.
- If your kids don't like vegetables (mine are never all that keen), try serving with a little bit of grated cheese on top.
- If you are adding nuts to any dish, toast them lightly in a frying pan before adding to the dish – you'll really notice the flavour boost!
- I'm a big fan of Vegeta, which is an all-round vegetable seasoning. I add it to things like chicken, popcorn, gravy – and my kids love the flavour.
- Mustard is delicious to flavour mayo in a salad dressing or stirred through macaroni and cheese.
- A teaspoon of curry powder is delicious in most chicken dishes and brings out the flavour in pumpkin soup.

How to s-t-r-e-t-c-h your meals

Shopping for the best deals on food and then storing and cooking it without wasting ingredients is great, but there is one more frugal trick you can use to make sure your dollar goes further – 'bulking out' meals. Now this doesn't mean they will be less nutritious – on the contrary, all of my tips are about *adding* nutrients!

- Add **grated vegetables** to everything! My children don't like vegetables, but I don't think they realise just how many vegetables they are really eating. When I pick fresh zucchini from the garden, it gets grated into everything. I do the same with carrots, mushrooms, broccoli and cauliflower. When searching for inspiration on how to get my kids to eat vegetables, I found a great book by Jessica Seinfeld (wife of Jerry). *Deceptively Delicious* was all about how to puree your vegetables and incorporate them into every meal. I tried it and it really worked! Of course, I don't have the time to puree all my vegetables these days (and the boys are way too old for that) – so grating is the answer!

- Add a can of drained **lentils** or some **rolled oats** to mince dishes such as patties, bolognaise, meatballs, pies – they give it a bit of texture, are super cheap, very good for you and the kids never know!

- Grab the big **potatoes** from the shops (I've seen white potatoes for as low as a $1 a kilo), bake them in the oven for an hour, and serve your meat in the baked potato! That way you don't need as much. And you can still serve steamed veggies on the side.

- Add **pearl barley** to soups and casseroles. It has a delicious nutty flavour and is a great way to thicken and extend dishes. It does take a few hours to cook though. (It's available from the soup section of the supermarket.)

- Use a **bread roll as a 'soup bowl'**. Cut off the top, pull out most of the bread (and turn that bread into croutons) – and pour the soup into the hollowed out bread roll!
- Use **rice noodles** (dried vermicelli and the flat noodles) to bulk out soups, and with stir-fries and other dishes.
- Make a quick **pasta salad** (cooked pasta, fresh vegetables and Greek-style yoghurt mixed together) as a side dish. Flavour with a little curry powder.
- Serve soup with **Toasted Cheesies** (bread topped with cheese and placed under the grill until lovely and melted; see recipe page 140).
- Serve everything with fresh crusty **bread**, or make some garlic or herb bread.
- If you know you can't stretch your main meal to fill tummies, serve a simple **appetiser** beforehand. It can be anything – cheese and crackers, Muffin Pizzas (page 164), or a simple soup.
- **Dessert** is another way to stretch a meal. I love Creamy Rice Pudding (page 308) as it's not only filling but simple and cheap to make.

Controlling your portions

Most of us probably don't realise, but we have been gradually increasing in the amount of food we load onto our plates, along with the corresponding increase in our waistlines. Drawing a connection between the two isn't exactly rocket science: we're not only eating way more food than our bodies need, but also eating too much of the wrong kinds of foods – foods that are high in calories (a.k.a processed carbs and sugars) and low in nutrients. In other words, we are overfed and undernourished. Aside from the enormous cost to our health (obesity, diabetes, heart disease), eating more than we need is just expensive.

The Australian Dietary Guidelines (updated in 2013) divide foods into different groups based on the nutrients they provide, and then recommend the number of serves of each group we need to eat to stay healthy. Each food group provides different nutrients, that's why we need to eat foods from *each* one and in balanced amounts.

Here's a rough idea of what adults are supposed to be eating, though note that kids and adolescents need an extra serve of grains and dairy foods each day. (The Nutrition Australia website has all the detailed info if you're interested.)

- Grains (cereal, bread, crackers, pasta, rice, etc.) = 6 serves.
- Vegetables = 5–6 serves.
- Fruit = 2 serves.
- Meat, eggs and vegetarian alternatives (beans, nuts, seeds) = 2½ serves.
- Milk, cheese, yoghurt and milk alternatives = 2½ serves.

Now, it is *super* important not to confuse 'serves' with 'portions'. For example, six serves of grains does not mean six *meals* worth of grains, but the total amount of grains that you should be eating every day. So, you might have two of them at breakfast, two at lunch and two at dinner. Here's what each serve really looks like:

GRAINS

This is the food group that gives us long-lasting energy, especially if we eat wholegrain versions of bread, pasta, etc. But most of us eat too much of it. I mean, have you ever read the serving sizes on a packet of cereal? Whenever I have cereal, I usually pour in at least half a bowl – but the actual serving size recommended on the pack is usually 30–40 grams. That's less than ½ cup, depending on the type of cereal! So even though cereal is cheap, easy and convenient, pay attention to the serving sizes.

1 serve = 1 slice of bread, ½ a bread roll, 30 g muesli, ½ cup cooked rice, pasta or porridge

VEGETABLES

The Australian Bureau of Statistics recently found that 92 per cent of us are not having the recommended five serves of vegetables every day.
1 serve = 1 cup of leafy veggies (like lettuce or spinach) or ½ cup of other veggies (potato, carrot, corn, etc.)

FRUIT

We're meant to have two serves a day.
1 serve = 1 medium-sized apple, banana or orange; or 2 apricots or kiwifruits

MEAT, EGGS AND VEGETARIAN ALTERNATIVES

Meat is probably the most complicated when it comes to serving sizes and portion control, especially here in Australia where we are big meat eaters. Most of us are supposed to have just 2½ serves a day, and you'll be amazed at how small the serving sizes are!
1 serve = 100 g red meat (or a steak the size of your palm); 120 g fish; 2 eggs; ½ cup legumes (cooked or canned); ⅓ cup nuts

DAIRY PRODUCTS

Milk, cheese and yoghurt contain calcium, a mineral that's really important for bone and muscle health, as well as a bunch of other vitamins and minerals. Most adults need 2½ serves a day, but if you're a woman over 50, it's recommended that you have 4 serves of diary products to help prevent osteoporosis.
1 serve = 250 ml milk; 200 g yoghurt, 40 g cheese

TREATS

These are obviously not important for health reasons, but we're only human so the dietary guidelines have included 1 serve of 'discretionary foods' per day. But wait for it . . .
1 serve of ice cream = two scoops (2 heaped tablespoons); 1 serve of chocolate = 25 g (four squares); 1 serve of hot chips = 12 chips (sob!); 1 serve of cake = a 40 g slice (that's without icing!)

My personal weakness is biscuits. It would be nothing for me to eat two or three shortbread bikkies with a cup of tea, which is way too much!

How to reduce your portions

Unfortunately, many of us have trained ourselves into thinking that unless we are totally 'stuffed', we are still hungry. You'll need to retrain your stomach (and brain) so that you stop eating when you feel satisfied – not when you're going to chunder!

A really simple way is to divide your food into four 'parts': one quarter should be meat or another protein (including dairy), one quarter should be grains (bread, rice, pasta) and the remaining half should be vegetables or salad. The great thing about eating more vegetables is that they are not only cheaper than proteins, but also bursting with vitamins, minerals and fibre, and it's the fibre that helps us to feel fuller.

Here are some other tricks of the trade when it comes to eating smaller portions:

- Serve your main meal on a side plate rather than a dinner plate.
- Serve your cereal in a small shallow bowl.
- Take your time eating – don't wolf it down. It takes your tummy 20 minutes to register that it is full!
- Buy a portion control plate from a dietitian or online – this makes it easy to 'dish out' exactly how much you should be eating.
- Distraction makes us eat more, so turn off the television at dinner time.
- Have a glass of water half an hour before you eat. And make sure you are drinking at least 2 litres of fluid per day (including water, tea, milk, etc.). Sometimes we think we're hungry, but we're really just dehydrated.
- Don't skip meals, especially lunch, otherwise you'll end up feeling so hungry by dinner time that you'll reach for anything!

The 10 Commandments of Successful Cooking

It's one thing to know the cheapest foods to buy, but you also need to know how best to store, prepare and cook them so that they taste delicious and you minimise waste. Here are my top tips for ensuring success in the kitchen.

1. Always read recipes from top to bottom *before* you go shopping or start cooking – there's nothing worse than getting halfway through a recipe and realising you're missing a key ingredient.
2. Make sure your fridge and pantry are stocked with the basics such as flour, eggs, butter, milk, rice, pasta, tinned tomatoes, etc. If you see staple items on sale – stock up.
3. Plan ahead. What part of this recipe may have leftovers to help with tomorrow's lunches or dinners? What is the best way to stretch this meal as far as you can? Most importantly, if you need to defrost ingredients take them out of the freezer the night before and leave them in the fridge to defrost. Then you have no excuse not to cook.
4. Use the correct measurements. (Yes, I've been known to throw things in here and there – and you can to a certain degree in savoury recipes – but desserts and cakes require precise measurements, so stick with what the recipes says.) And if you are doubling quantities remember to add a tiny bit more liquid as scaling up desserts can make them dry.
5. Clean dishes and benchtops as you go. Dishwashers are invaluable – they actually use less water than the sink – and to be quite frank, when you are doing lots of cooking, washing up by hand totally sucks. (Of course, if you don't mind washing up by hand, I'm not going to judge you!)

Whatever method you use, get into the habit of leaving a clean kitchen before going to bed so you wake up with a fresh slate. That mindset at the start of the day is invaluable.

6. Use a timer for your recipes so you don't turn all your hard work to charcoal! If you don't have a kitchen timer on your stove or oven, use your phone!

7. Make notes next to the recipe about how you might improve it next time. Does it need more seasoning? Were the potatoes under done? Every oven is different and although it might work perfectly in my oven, it may be slightly different in yours.

8. Check the freshness of your ingredients before you start. Eggs can be easily tested for freshness in a glass of water (page 103). In fact, I always crack eggs into a cup, and then add them to the recipe just to make sure – nothing worse than having a cake recipe nearly done and adding a bad egg!

9. Get to know your oven and microwave, as they are all different. Gas and electric ovens cook differently. Some have hot spots, cold spots. Some heat too fast or some need a long time to heat up to the right temperature. The more cooking you do, the better you will get.

10. Last of all – sometimes disasters can turn into the most wonderful of recipes. I once went to make a caramel and oreo slice. I totally stuffed up the recipe and it turned into a sloppy mess so I left it covered on the oven and walked away. A few hours later, I saw that the whole thing had caramelised and when sliced was perhaps the tastiest and most delicious recipe I'd ever tried – so the gooey condensed milk slice was born! Overdone cakes can be put in a food processor and used as crumbs for delicious things like fried ice cream.

CHAPTER 5:

Growing your own food

I SIMPLY ADORE GARDENING. There is nothing better than being outside and getting your hands dirty. Creating your own vegetable garden is a great way to save money and to ensure that you and your family are eating the healthiest food possible. And if your kids are fussy with vegetables, get them out there helping you to water and harvest them – children are much more likely to eat veggies when they have put some love and care into tending them.

If you have a brown thumb, keep the garden small to start off with. Only grow plants that you know will be eaten. You don't need a huge space to grow your own food – you can grow herbs, tomatoes and lettuces in pots. But if you are lucky enough to have a bit of ground space, be daring and try a few things. Lettuce and tomatoes are a good place to start. Once you have mastered those – then go on to experiment with other vegetables. Zucchini are easy to grow, too, so are popular for people just starting out. I have a bit of land so I like to grow around ten broccoli plants each season. That way, I can blanch and freeze the excess to use throughout the year.

Starting off a veggie patch

Even though seeds are the most economical choice to start a vegetable patch with, if you are a beginner, it is probably best to start with a punnet of seedlings – they are a lot easier to manage.

Make sure you have good soil in your garden bed, and that the plants will receive plenty of sunshine and water. Vegetables are 'hungry' plants, and need regular fertilising or they just won't produce much. So either use a prescribed fertiliser from the local shop (which is expensive) or start a compost heap.

What you decide to grow will depend on the climate where you live. I live in the subtropics, not too far from the coast, so I can grow things like lettuce and tomatoes in autumn and winter. If you are in a temperate area like south-east Australia, high up on a mountain, or in a drier inland area, what you can grow will vary. There is lots of fantastic planting information online, though personally, I do love my *Yates Garden Guide*.

Herbs are a great addition to any vegetable patch and they beat any dried varieties that can be bought in the spice section hands down. You can easily grow mint, oregano, sage, thyme, marjoram and rosemary. Basil and coriander are annuals, so to enjoy them all year round, I freeze the ones I've grown in spring and summer. To do this, I process them in a food processor with a little olive oil, spoon the mixture into ice cubes and freeze. Then I pop the frozen herb blocks into a zip-lock bag and date it. Whenever I need a bit of 'something something' in a casserole or soup, I just pop in a herb ice-block!

Re-growing food

There are loads of common vegetable and fruit scraps that can be re-grown – effectively giving you food for free! You'll have the most success with organically grown fruit and veggies (which, yes, are usually a bit more expensive) – or vegetables sold at the local markets.

LEEKS, SPRING ONIONS AND FENNEL

When you cut off the bases, plant them root-first into good soil in a garden bed (for temperate areas) or pot (if you're in the subtropics), or if you live in a colder area, start them inside on a windowsill and move them outside when they're established. Within 3–5 days you should begin to see new growth coming up. Remember to water and fertilise regularly to keep the plant healthy. Remove the produce as you need it and just leave the roots in the soil to continually harvest your kitchen scrap crops.

LETTUCE AND CABBAGE

You'll need a whole lettuce or cabbage to start with, preferably organic or from a local market. Cut off the base and plant it stalk-side down into well-fertilised soil in a sunny position. Keep it well watered, and in a few weeks, your new plant will be ready for harvest. You can regrow it from the white root end again and again.

GINGER AND HORSERADISH

These are possibly the easiest scraps to re-grow. Both ginger and horseradish are very forgiving. Just take a chunk from either and place it directly into the soil. Make sure the newest buds are facing upwards. These plants enjoy partly shaded areas rather than full sun. Ginger also makes for a very attractive indoor plant.

POTATOES AND SWEET POTATOES

You can grow any variety of potato you like provided that it has an 'eye' on it. Chop off a good chunk of the potato with the eye and leave it to dry out at room temperature for a couple of days. Leaving the pieces to dry a little will cause them to form a type of 'scab' over the cut end, which will prevent the potato from rotting in the ground.

Plant the potato cubes about 10 cm deep and make sure that the soil below the roots is *really* loose. Water with a fine spray. As the plant dies down a few months later, go digging for the potato gold that will be in the soil!

GARLIC

You only need a single clove of garlic to regrow an entire garlic plant. And garlic plants are wonderful at keeping away pests in your vegetable patch or near a rose garden! Place the clove of garlic in a warm part of your home without direct sunlight. Very soon it should 'shoot' and will start growing roots.

Plant in good quality soil. When the top browns off, you will find a head of garlic underneath and you can harvest it and start the whole process all over again!

PINEAPPLES

Pineapples are from the same family as bromeliads and are very easy to regrow. Cut off the leafy 'head' of the pineapple and pull away the fruity bit until you see the fleshy root. Plant the leafy head into good quality soil (in a pot if you like) and water regularly. Okay, so it takes about two years before the pineapple will produce fruit, but it is an attractive (and free) plant to grow in the meantime.

Tip from a SAHM

A great old-fashioned trick is to place a garbage bag with rotting apples around the pineapple plant at about two years old – the fermentation of the apples will release a gas to trick the pineapple into fruiting sooner.

CHAPTER 6:
Making your own staples

There are many products that we buy week in,
week out at the supermarket that we can easily make
at home – and save lots of money in the process.
Sure, it will take more time, but that's to be expected
when you are saving money. And there is something
sublime about being in the kitchen, knowing exactly
what is going into your family's food.

Homemade mayo

Salad dressings are so easy to make and can totally transform a boring meal. It's great making something that can add so much flavour to your food without it being full of crappy preservatives and other additives.

Makes about 1 cup

2 egg yolks

1 tablespoon vinegar

pepper, to taste

1 cup olive oil

Place the egg yolks, vinegar and pepper in a food processor or blender (you can also make it in a bowl with a stick blender). Process for 10–15 seconds or until the mixture is well combined. With the motor still running, slowly add the olive oil in a thin stream until the mixture is thick and creamy. If you like your mayo a bit thinner, stir in a few drops of hot water. Transfer to a sealed container and refrigerate for up to 4 days.

No-egg mayo

This is a sweet and sour dressing that is especially delicious with coleslaw or potato salad.

Makes 2 cups

1 × 395 ml tin sweetened condensed milk (see recipe page 99)

200 ml brown malt vinegar

2 teaspoons dijon mustard

Place all of the ingredients in a large jar and shake well to combine. Store leftovers (covered with a lid) in the fridge for up to 5 days.

Basic vinaigrette

You'll never need to buy dressing again – this is so easy!

Makes ¾ cup

½ cup olive oil

¼ cup brown malt vinegar

salt and pepper to taste

Place the ingredients in a jar with a lid. Shake well and serve over a crisp salad. Refrigerate leftover dressing for up to 4 days.

Italian herb dressing

If you make this one with fresh herbs from the garden, it will be even more delicious.

Makes ¾ cup

2 teaspoons dried Italian herbs (oregano, basil, marjoram, thyme, rosemary)

½ cup olive oil

¼ cup brown malt vinegar

Place all of the ingredients in a jar, seal and shake well. Leave for an hour or so for the flavours to infuse. Will keep in a jar in the fridge for up to 4 days.

Thousand island dressing

Although traditionally used for seafood, this dressing is delicious with chicken or pork.

Makes 1 cup

¾ cup mayo
(see recipe page 80)

1 cup tomato sauce

2 teaspoons
Worcestershire sauce

3 teaspoons white pepper

Mix all the ingredients in a small bowl until well combined. Serve with any seafood dish. If you have any leftovers, store in a sealed container in the fridge for up to 4 days.

Tomato pasta sauce

Another staple that is cheap and easy to make.

Makes about 2 × 500 ml jars or bottles

2 tablespoons olive oil

1 onion, finely chopped

1 garlic clove, crushed

1 tablespoon red wine vinegar

3 × 400 g cans crushed tomatoes

¼ cup tomato paste

1 teaspoon dried basil

1 teaspoon dried oregano

Heat the olive oil in a heavy-based saucepan over medium heat. Add the onion and garlic and cook for about 5–6 minutes until the onion is lightly golden. Add the vinegar and tomatoes and simmer, uncovered, for 25 minutes, stirring occasionally.

Meanwhile, sterilise the bottles or jars by running them through a hot cycle in the dishwasher (or washing them thoroughly in very hot soapy water, rinsing and then drying them in the oven).

Add the tomato paste and herbs to the sauce and simmer for a further 15 minutes to reduce. Pour into the sterilised jars or bottles. Allow to cool and store in the fridge.

Sweet chilli sauce

This is so simple to make and so delicious!

Makes about 3 × 500 ml jars or bottles

500 g red cayenne chillies, halved lengthways and seeds removed

4 teaspoons crushed garlic

3 cups white wine vinegar

3 cups caster sugar

Place the chillies and garlic in a food processor with 1 cup of vinegar. Pulse until very finely chopped, but not pureed.

Transfer the chilli mixture to a heavy-based saucepan over a medium–high heat. Add the sugar and the remaining vinegar and cook for a few minutes, stirring constantly, until the sugar is dissolved. Cover and simmer for 35–40 minutes or until the mixture reduces and thickens.

Meanwhile, sterilise the bottles or jars by running them through a hot cycle in the dishwasher (or washing them thoroughly in very hot soapy water, rinsing and then drying them in the oven).

Pour into the sterilised jars or bottles and seal. Once you open a bottle, keep it in the fridge so it lasts longer.

Satay sauce

This sauce is absolutely delicious served over baked chicken pieces, fish or steamed veggies, and always tastes so much better than any shop-bought variety.

Makes 1½ cups

1 tablespoon olive oil

1 teaspoon crushed garlic

1 onion, chopped finely

¼ teaspoon chilli powder (optional)

½ cup crunchy peanut butter

1 tablespoon soy sauce

1 tablespoon lemon juice

1 tablespoon brown sugar

¾ cup coconut cream

salt and pepper

Heat the olive oil in a saucepan over medium heat. Add the garlic, onion and chilli powder (if using) and cook until the onion is just soft and clear (about 5 minutes). Add the peanut butter, soy sauce, lemon juice and brown sugar and stir until the sugar is melted and everything is well combined.

Take the mixture off the heat and stir in the coconut cream. Place back on the heat and cook until the mixture boils, stirring constantly.

Season to taste with salt and pepper and serve immediately. The sauce will keep well in a sealed container in the fridge for up to 3 days.

Basic gravy

When it comes to making gravy, many people reach for packet mixes, but it's actually very simple to make from scratch.

roasting pan juices
(or 2 stock cubes, any kind)

3 tablespoons plain flour

If you have just cooked a roast, transfer the meat to a plate or dish, cover with foil and allow to rest for 5 minutes. Meanwhile, carefully pour off any excess fat from the juices in the roasting pan and return the pan to medium heat. Add any extra juices from the standing plate.

Alternatively, place the stock cubes and ¼ cup of water in a saucepan over medium heat.

Heat the roasting pan (or saucepan) until the mixture is bubbling. Add the flour, stirring continuously, until the flour absorbs all the juices and no longer tastes 'floury'. Add a cup of water at a time until you get the consistency you require.

Serve immediately over roast meat and vegetables, in a cold meat wrap, with chips or however you love your gravy!

Creamy mustard sauce

A delicious sauce that is perfect with all kinds of meat.

Makes 1½ cups

roasting pan juices

1 teaspoon butter

1 teaspoon crushed garlic

¼ cup white wine or chicken stock

2 tablespoons wholegrain mustard

1 teaspoon dried thyme

300 ml cream

salt and pepper

First cook the meat you plan on serving with the sauce and remove from the pan. Pour off any excess fat, leaving behind the juices. Return the pan to medium heat. Add the butter and garlic and fry off for about a minute. Add the white wine or stock, mustard and thyme. Turn up the heat and add the cream. Simmer for 5 minutes or until the sauce has thickened. Season if needed. Spoon over the meat and serve right away.

Hummus

A delicious, healthy dip. If you like, you can smooth out the flavour by adding some Greek-style yoghurt.

Makes 1 cup

1 × 400 g can chickpeas, drained and rinsed

1 clove garlic, crushed

1 tablespoon lemon juice

3 tablespoons tahini

pinch of ground cumin

big pinch of salt

In a food processor, puree the chickpeas and garlic to a stiff paste. Add the lemon juice, tahini, cumin, salt and 2 tablespoons of water and process for 1–2 minutes or until smooth and creamy. Add more water if necessary to achieve the desired consistency. Store in the fridge in a sealed container for up to 4 days. This dip freezes well, too.

Hints & Tips

∗ Tahini (sesame seed paste) lasts for ages in the fridge, so even though it might seem expensive to start with, you end up being able to make many batches of hummus.

Pesto

So versatile! Serve as a dip, as a pasta sauce or as a delicious topping for pizza. This is a great way to use homegrown basil leaves.

Makes about 2 cups

2 cups basil leaves

60 g cashews, lightly toasted

2 cloves garlic, coarsely chopped

big pinch of salt

⅓ cup olive oil

½ cup grated parmesan

Place the basil, cashews, garlic, salt and oil in a food processor and blitz to a chunky puree. Remove the blade and stir through the cheese. Serve over fresh pasta, or spread over your favourite pizza base.

Hints & Tips

✳ Pesto freezes well. Spoon into greased ice cube trays, cover with plastic wrap and freeze for up to 3 months. (Or pop the cubes out of the trays when frozen and transfer to zip-locks or another freezer-proof container.)

Caramelised onions

It's hard to believe that a veggie that makes you cry when you chop it, can turn into such a sweet and delectable food! Caramelised onions are delicious on pizzas, in burgers, or added to wraps with leftover meats. They are also fabulous spooned over a salad.

4 onions (brown, red or white), finely sliced into rings

2 tablespoons butter

1 tablespoon brown sugar

1 tablespoon balsamic vinegar

Heat the butter in a heavy-based frying pan over medium heat until it's bubbling. Add the onion rings and cook for 10–12 minutes, stirring occasionally, until very soft. Stir in the brown sugar and balsamic vinegar and cook a further 5 minutes or until syrupy and caramelised.

Hints & Tips

* If you're not using all of the onions now, transfer them to a very clean jar – they should keep well in the fridge for up to a week. You can freeze them, too, for up to 3 months.

Tzatziki

Tzatziki is not only a lovely light sauce over chicken or fish, but also makes a delicious dip for chopped veggies, crackers and even hot chips. It stores well in the fridge for up to a week.

Makes 3 cups

3 small cucumbers, coarsely grated

500 g Greek-style yoghurt

3 teaspoons crushed garlic

1 teaspoon dried dill

1 tablespoon extra virgin olive oil, plus extra to serve

salt and pepper

Line a colander with cheesecake cloth or muslin. Place the grated cucumber in the centre of the cloth and draw up the sides, squeezing firmly to remove as much moisture as possible. Transfer the cucumber to a mixing bowl. Add the yoghurt, garlic, dill and olive oil and mix well. Season to taste, cover and place in the fridge overnight for the flavours to develop. To serve, place a small amount in a bowl and lightly drizzle with extra virgin olive oil.

Easy garlic croutons

Croutons are brilliant in soups and salads, and are a great way to use up stale bread. These are made with garlic, but you can also use herbs if you prefer.

Serves 4

3 tablespoons olive oil

3 teaspoons crushed garlic

4 slices of bread

Preheat the oven to 210°C.

Place the olive oil and garlic on a baking tray and stir to combine. Place the tray in the oven to heat.

While the oil is heating, cut the bread into 1 cm cubes. When the oil is starting to spit, remove the tray from the oven and add the croutons, stirring to coat. Pop back into the oven for 5 minutes or until they are crispy and golden. Serve immediately.

Homemade bread rolls

I've made these in a muffin tray (they look so cute!) but you can just pop them on a greased and dusted baking tray if you prefer.

Makes 12

2 cups plain flour

½ teaspoon salt (optional)

1 teaspoon sugar

1 sachet yeast (7 g)

1 egg, lightly beaten

2 tablespoons butter, melted and cooled

¾ cup warm water

canola oil spray

Place the flour, salt, sugar and yeast in a large bowl and mix well. Add the beaten egg, butter and warm water and mix together to make a stiff dough. Place the dough in an oiled bowl, cover with plastic wrap and keep in a warm place until the dough has doubled in size.

Preheat the oven to 200°C and grease a 12-hole muffin tray with canola oil spray.

Punch down the dough and divide it into twelve equal portions. Form each portion into a ball and place it in the muffin tray. Leave in a warm place until the dough has risen to the top of the tins. Bake for 15–20 minutes or until golden brown.

Homemade oat flour

Oats are naturally gluten free (but do double check the packaging – they may be processed on the same equipment as wheat or rye). However, since oat flour doesn't contain any gluten (the protein that gives wheat its elasticity), when you use it for baking, you'll need to mix it with some gluten-free wheat flour as well or you'll end up with a great big lump of oat brick!

Makes 500 g

500 g oats, any kind (rolled, quick or steel cut, see page 13)

Place the oats in a high-powered blender or food processor. Blend until the oats resemble a fine powder. Seal the flour in one or two zip-lock bags and keep in the freezer until needed.

Homemade tortillas

I actually love tortillas, probably more than bread, and they make an easy and cheap substitute for wraps. They're also fantastic pizza bases . . . so many uses!

Makes about 10

3 cups plain flour

½ teaspoon salt

1 teaspoon baking powder

⅓ cup vegetable oil

1 cup warm milk

canola oil spray

Sift the flour, salt and baking powder into a large bowl. Make a well in the centre and add the oil and milk and mix with a wooden spoon until combined. Transfer to a floured surface and knead until the mixture comes together and becomes smooth.

Divide the dough into about 10 equal portions and roll each into a rough ball. Tear off 10 sheets of baking paper about 25 cm × 25 cm. Place a ball between two sheets of the paper and use a rolling pin to roll it into a circle 20–25 cm in diameter and 2 mm thick. Set the tortilla aside, removing the top sheet of baking paper to use for the next tortilla. Repeat with the remaining dough until you have a stack of tortillas separated with sheets of baking paper. Place tortillas in the fridge to rest for 30 minutes.

If you don't want to cook them straight away, place the uncooked tortillas (still separated with baking paper) in a plastic bag in the freezer, where they'll keep well for 2 months.

Hints & Tips

✳ If you are cooking frozen tortillas, you don't need to defrost them first.

To cook the fresh tortillas, heat a frying pan to medium heat and spray with canola oil spray. Fry each tortilla for 2 minutes on each side or until evenly browned and cooked through. They taste best on the day they are cooked.

Shortcrust pastry

Making your own pastry might sound a bit fussy, but it's actually quite fun and very satisfying. Don't skimp on the butter – it's the key to a crumbly, delicious crust.

Serves 4

1½ cups flour

½ teaspoon salt

100 g cold butter, cut into cubes

iced water

Place the flour in a mixing bowl with the salt and butter. Using your fingertips, rub the butter into the flour until the mixture looks like coarse breadcrumbs. Stir in the iced water, 1 tablespoon at a time, until the dough just comes to together.

Turn out onto a sheet of plastic wrap or baking paper, and cover with another sheet. Use a rolling pin to roll out to about 3 mm thick. (You can skip the paper or plastic and just flour the bench and rolling pin if you prefer.) Cut to fit the top of your pie dish, ramekins etc, and use as per the recipe.

Homemade English muffins

Some people are afraid to work with yeast, but it's really not that hard. You just need to make sure the water is only just warm, otherwise the hot water will kill the yeast. I use a scone cutter for my muffins, but you could use a teacup or a small glass.

Makes 12

1 cup milk

1 cup warm water

1 sachet dry yeast (7 g)

2 tablespoons honey

¼ cup butter or margarine, melted

1 teaspoon salt

6 cups plain flour

polenta for dusting

canola oil spray for cooking and greasing

In a small saucepan heat the milk over medium heat until it starts to form tiny bubbles at the edges of the pan. Remove from the heat, transfer to a large mixing bowl and allow to cool to lukewarm.

Meanwhile, dissolve the yeast in the warm water. Stir in the honey and let the mixture stand for 10 minutes or until the yeast starts to activate (a layer of bubbly froth will form at the top). Add the yeast mixture to the milk. Stir in the melted butter and salt. Gradually add the flour, mixing until a soft dough forms. Knead for a minute, place in a greased bowl, cover and allow to rise (about 1 hour).

Punch down the dough and turn out onto a floured surface. Roll out and cut with scone cutters. Dust with polenta and place on a greased tray. Place in a warm spot and leave the dough to rise for another hour.

To cook your muffins, heat a large heavy-based frying pan over medium heat and spray with a little canola oil spray. Cook the muffins in batches for about 10 minutes on each side.

Eat while hot with butter and honey!

Homemade crumpets

Make these on the weekend for a delicious treat!

Makes 6

7 g dry yeast

2 cups warm water

1 cup plain flour

1 teaspoon salt

2 tablespoons butter,
plus extra for greasing

In a bowl or jug, mix the yeast with ¼ cup of the warm water and stir until the yeast is dissolved. Leave it for 5 minutes to do its frothy thing.

In a separate bowl, sift the flour and salt. Whisk 1½ cups of the remaining warm water into the flour then add the yeast mixture, stirring until combined.

Cover and leave the mixture in a warm place until it doubles in size (about 1 hour). The mixture should be quite thick but still pour easily. Add more of the remaining warm water if the mixture is too thick to pour.

Lightly grease two egg rings with the extra butter.

Heat 2 teaspoons of the butter in a frying pan over a medium–low heat. Place the rings in the pan and pour in batter until each ring is about half full. Cook for about 4 minutes or until small holes appear on the tops of the crumpets. Remove the ring, flip the crumpets and cook a further minute until golden. Set aside and keep warm. Repeat with the remaining butter and mixture.

Butter lightly while hot and serve with honey or jam.

Naan bread

This recipe is not only a great accompaniment to curries and casseroles, but is also terrific as a pizza base.

Makes 8

1½ cups warm water

1 tablespoon sugar

15 g (or 2 sachets) dry yeast

1 teaspoon salt

3 cups plain flour, sifted

canola oil spray

In a bowl mix together the warm water, sugar and yeast. Allow to stand for 5 minutes or until it starts to go foamy as the yeast activates.

Add the salt and fold in the sifted flour. Knead well on a floured work surface and form into a tight ball. Place the dough in a well oiled bowl, cover with a damp tea towel and allow it to rise (30–45 minutes).

Turn the dough onto a floured workspace and divide it into 8 even portions. Use a rolling pin to roll out each portion to an oval shape about 4 mm thick.

Heat a heavy-based frying pan over medium heat and lightly grease with canola oil spray. Pan-fry the bread for 1–2 minutes until nicely browned. Serve fresh and hot.

Homemade slow-cooker yoghurt

I love making my own yoghurt. It takes a while, but is just so creamy and delicious. You can use skim milk if you prefer, but it won't thicken as well as full-cream milk.

Makes 4 cups

2 litres full-cream milk

½ cup plain, Greek-style yoghurt (you need a starter!)

Turn your slow cooker onto the low setting and add all of the milk. Cover and heat for 2½ hours. Turn off the slow cooker, leave the lid on and let it sit for 3 hours.

Transfer 2 cups of the warm milk to a jug. Add the yoghurt and stir gently until well combined. Pour the yoghurt mixture into the slow cooker and stir well. Replace the lid and wrap the cooker in a towel or blanket (this is for insulation). Let the mixture sit for 8 hours.

Scoop the yoghurt into a plastic container, add the flavouring of your choice and refrigerate.

Homemade butter

Technically speaking, it isn't actually cheaper to make your own butter. However, if you find yourself with extra cream sitting in your fridge, this is a great way to use it up. There is nothing on this earth like homemade butter on freshly made bread, with just a smidge of Vegemite . . . drool!

Makes ½ cup

400 ml cream

salt to taste

Place the cream in your stand mixer and, starting on low, gradually increase the speed until the mixture looks like scrambled eggs. (This can take 5–15 minutes depending on the amount of fat in your cream.) Drain off the liquid and keep it for making scones, pancakes or anything that calls for milk (waste nothing!). Stir in a pinch of salt (or to taste) and place the butter in a sealed jar. It will keep well in the fridge for 2–3 days, and in the freezer for up to 6 months.

Sweetened condensed milk

Sweetened condensed milk truly is the nectar of the gods. I could just open a can and drink the lot! Here's how to make it at home if you run out.

Makes about 2 cups

1 cup milk

2 eggs

1 cup brown sugar

1 teaspoon vanilla essence

2 tablespoons plain flour

½ teaspoon baking powder

¼ teaspoon salt

Combine all of the ingredients in a bowl or jug and mix well. Use immediately in any recipe that calls for sweetened condensed milk, such as my Bulk Biscuits (page 268) or Coconut Macaroons (page 270).

Dairy- and egg-free sweetened condensed milk

As I have a fair few recipes with sweetened condensed milk, I thought it would be great to give an alternative for people who can't eat eggs or dairy.

Makes 5 cups

3 cups soy milk

3 cups white sugar

3 tablespoons cornflour, sifted

Place the soy milk and sugar in a saucepan over a medium–low heat, stir gently until the sugar dissolves. Turn the heat to low and simmer for 20 minutes (don't let it boil) until the soy milk has reduced. Remove from the heat.

Place the cornflour in a small cup with 1 tablespoon of water and mix to a thick paste. Pour the cornflour mixture into the heated milk and whisk until thickened. Transfer to an airtight jar or sealed container and refrigerate. It will last for up to 4 days.

Sugar-free condensed milk

If you are trying to cut down on sugar, this is a great option.

Makes 1½ cups

1 cup powdered milk

⅔ cup stevia or other sugar substitute

⅓ cup boiled water

3 teaspoons melted butter

Place all the ingredients in a bowl and beat until smooth. This mixture will keep in a sealed container in the fridge for 2 days.

Homemade cottage cheese

Even though making your own cottage cheese works out roughly the same cost as buying a generic brand from a supermarket, the taste is incomparable – plus you get the satisfaction of knowing exactly what's going into your food! This is delicious on toast with some jam or sliced banana for breakfast, or made into Spinach Slice (page 209).

Makes 500 g

2 litres milk (you can use skim milk if you desire)

4 tablespoons white vinegar

salt to taste

Pour the milk into a large saucepan and heat gently over medium heat until you see small bubbles forming at the edges. Remove from the heat and add the white vinegar. Stir gently until curds start to form, then leave the mixture to sit for about 20 minutes.

Line a colander with a piece of muslin and place it over a bowl. Pour the curds into the colander and allow to drain for 1 hour. Reserve the whey (place it in a sealed container in the fridge or freezer, and use it in smoothies or any recipe that calls for buttermilk).

Transfer the curds to a glass bowl or container, cover and pop in the fridge. Cottage cheese will last in the fridge for up to 4 days.

Slow-cooked chicken stock

Always collect chicken carcasses and bones when you use chicken and place them in a bag in the freezer for when you decide to make a bulk lot of chicken stock – which is always much nicer and less salty than the shop-bought versions. Plus you can freeze it so it can always be on hand!

Makes 2 litres

2 kg chicken bones or carcasses

2–3 brown onions, peeled and quartered

4 carrots, trimmed and roughly chopped

½ bunch celery (including base and stalks), roughly chopped

2 tablespoons crushed garlic

2 bay leaves (optional)

1 teaspoon salt

Place the chicken bones on an oven tray and bake for 45 minutes or until browned. Transfer to the slow cooker together with the remaining ingredients and cover with water. Cook on low for 8 hours.

Place a sieve over a bowl and strain the liquid, discarding the vegetables. Allow the stock to cool to room temperature. Cover and refrigerate overnight.

In the morning, remove any fat that has solidified on the top. Pour the stock into ice cube trays or cleaned butter containers and freeze for up to 6 months.

Some brilliant food prep hacks

Softening ice cream: Ever taken out ice cream and found it is just way too hard to scoop? Well keep your ice cream container sealed in an extra large zip-lock bag in the freezer. It will always be easily scoop-able.

Cutting onions: Always place your onion in the freezer for 15 minutes before chopping. This will stop your eyes from watering.

Peeling egg shells: Place the boiled egg in a small glass jar. Put the lid on and give it a good shake. The shell will crack and loosen so you can peel it off easily without damaging the egg.

Making crystal clear ice cubes: For clear beautiful ice cubes, freeze boiled water. Room temperature water always ends up making cloudy ice cubes.

Testing if eggs are rotten: To see if an egg is still good or not, place it in a tall glass of water. If it floats, throw it out. If it sinks to the bottom it is fresh and still good to use.

Removing bits of egg shell: If you've cracked eggs into a bowl and a tiny piece of shell has fallen in, the best way to remove it is to use a bigger piece of the shell. The shell pieces are 'attracted' to each other (like magnets), which makes it easy to pick up the little one.

Separating egg yolks from egg whites: Crack the egg into a small bowl. Hold a clean, empty plastic drink bottle (top removed) over the cracked egg. Squeeze the bottle to create a small vacuum, gently place the bottle neck on the yolk and 'suck it up'.

Opening a jar: Turn the jar upside down and 'bang' the lid (not too hard) on the counter top – it should now open easily!

Softening butter: Grate hard butter with a cheese grater – it makes it more pliable in minutes.

Preventing pots boiling over: Place a wooden spoon across the top of a pot – it will never boil over it!

Slicing meat very finely: If you want extra-fine slices of meat for your stir-fry, use a very sharp knife and slice the meat while it is partly frozen.

Keeping your kitchen sponges germ-free: Every night when you put the dishwasher on, pop your sponge or cloth in the top drawer of your dishwasher. The heat and soap will sterilise and make your kitchen cloths as good as new and ready for the next day.

CHAPTER 7:

Three meal plans

Here are three examples of meal plans,
along with a rough list of the ingredients you
would need to make most of the suggested recipes
for the week. Of course you can't make every recipe
I've listed – I just wanted to show you the range
of dishes you could make with limited ingredients.
Choose the ones you want, and you will
easily come under budget!

The 'Family of Four' Plan

This was the very first $50 shop meal plan that I made public. I would change the recipes each week, but the staples were pretty much the same.

SHOPPING LIST

MEAT
750 g bacon
500 g beef mince
1 kg chicken pieces

DAIRY
500 g butter
3 L milk

FRUIT AND VEG
6 apples
2 kg brushed potatoes
1 head broccoli
1 kg onions
1 small packet sultanas

TINNED AND FROZEN
3 tins crushed tomatoes
1 kg frozen mixed vegetables
1 tin sweetcorn kernels

PANTRY
18 eggs
2 loaves bread
500g long grain rice
1 packet French onion soup mix
2 packets spaghetti
150 g popping corn
1 kg rolled oats
1 kg self-raising flour
2 vegetable stock cubes

MEAL OPTIONS

Breakfast

Breakfast Rice (page 120)
Good Ol' Porridge (page 114)
Homemade Hash Browns
  (page 134)

Homemade Pancakes or Waffles
  (page 124)
Perfect Scrambled Eggs
  (page 120)

Lunch

Corn Fritters (page 129)
Egg and Bacon English Muffins
  (page 121)

French Toast (page 119)
Spaghetti Omelette (page 132)
Stuffed Sweet Potatoes (page 201)

Dinner

Fried Rice (page 182)
Slow-cooker Apricot Chicken
  (page 264)
Toasted Cheesies (page 140)

Traditional Aussie Rissoles
  (page 244)
Traditional Spaghetti Bolognaise
  (page 248)

Dessert

Creamy Rice Pudding (page 308)

Real Vanilla Custard (page 306)
  with baked apples

Snacks

Apple and Oat Muffins (page 278)

Savoury Popcorn (page 155)

The 'Student Living on Nothing' Plan

This might suit someone who has just moved out of home and is studying and working part-time, with not much time to prepare meals.

SHOPPING LIST

MEAT

500 g beef mince
1 chicken breast
100 g shredded ham

DAIRY

250 g butter
1 L milk
250 g tasty cheese

FRUIT AND VEG

1 kg potatoes
1 small packet sultanas

TINNED AND FROZEN

500 g frozen mixed vegetables
1 tin evaporated milk
1 large tin salmon
1 tin sweetcorn kernels

PANTRY

6 eggs
1 jar of jam
1 loaf of bread
4 packets chicken two-minute noodles
1 packet French onion soup
1 packet jelly crystals
1 kg rolled oats
1 kg self-raising flour

MEAL OPTIONS

Breakfast
....

Boiled Eggs on Toast (page 118)
Dairy- and Egg-free Sultana
    Pancakes (page 126)
Good Ol' Porridge (page 114)

Hot Potato Breakfast Fry-up
    (page 125)
Perfect Scrambled Eggs (page 120)

Lunch
....

Cheese Sandwich Soufflé
    (page 150)
Chicken Noodle Omelette
    (page 128)

French Toast (page 119)
Impossible Pie (page 183)
Toasted Cheesies (page 140)

Dinner
....

Corn Fritters (page 129)
    with steamed vegetables
Meatloaf in a Mug (page 166)
Quiche in a Cup (page 165)

Salmon Patties (page 157)
    with steamed vegetables
Traditional Aussie Rissoles
    (page 244)

Dessert
....

Jelly Whip (page 309)
Old-Fashioned Steamed Pudding
    (page 320)

Slow-cooker Bread and Butter
    Pudding (page 310)

The 'Hungry Horde of Kids' Plan

This is for larger families, so will have to come in at more than $50 per week – but is still a great way to save money and fill hungry tummies.

SHOPPING LIST

MEAT

1 kg bacon
2 kg chicken pieces
1 kg gravy beef
2 kg mince

DAIRY

500 g butter
4 L milk
250 g tasty cheese

FRUIT AND VEG

1 kg apples
2 kg potatoes
2 kg sweet potatoes

TINNED AND FROZEN

1 kg frozen mixed vegetables
1 packet puff pastry sheets
1 tin cannellini beans

PANTRY

2 kg bread mix
100 g cocoa
24 eggs
1 kg flour
4 packets two-minute noodles
1 packet veg stock cubes
1 kg rolled oats
2 kg rice
1 kg spaghetti

MEAL OPTIONS

Breakfast

Breakfast Rice (page 120)
Good Ol' Porridge (page 114)
Homemade Pancakes (page 124)

Homemade Waffles (page 124)
Perfect Scrambled Eggs (page 120)

Lunch

Egg and Bacon English Muffins
  (page 121)
Boiled Eggs (page 118) on toast
French Toast (page 119)

Homemade Hash Browns
  (page 134)
Spaghetti Omelette (page 132)

Dinner

Easy Sausage Rolls (page 146)
Fried Rice (page 182)
Slow-cooker Apricot Chicken
  (page 264)

Stuffed Sweet Potatoes (page 201)
Traditional Spaghetti Bolognaise
  (page 248)

Dessert

Creamy Rice Pudding (page 308)
Homemade Chocolate Pudding
  (page 302)

Real Vanilla Custard (page 306)
  with baked apples

Snacks

Apple and Oat Muffins (page 278)

Savoury Popcorn (page 155)

FRUGAL RECIPES

Breakfast

People can be tempted to skimp on breakfast, but it's actually the most important meal of the day. Younger children often prefer cereal, which is great for frugal parents as the cheapest cereals are usually the healthiest options (oats, wheat biscuits, puffed rice). Don't give your kids the sugary, processed ones — plain cereal is great with some chopped banana, a drizzle of honey or a few berries. And don't be scared of using generic-brand cereal — it is often made in exactly the same factory with exactly the same ingredients. Just make sure you seal it well or keep it in an airtight container so that it stays fresh. Also, only give the kids a little bit of cereal at a time — they can always ask for more if they are still hungry. Otherwise you end up throwing out a soggy mess — and that is wastage! Less is more!

Good ol' porridge

Porridge is one of my favourite breakfasts. I love to create my own individually flavoured porridge sachets to make things even easier. I just place each serve in a zip-lock bag and store it in the pantry to keep it fresh.

Serves 1

½ cup quick oats

2 teaspoons brown sugar (optional)

tiny pinch of salt

1 tablespoon of flavouring (e.g. coconut, cinnamon, sultanas, chopped walnuts, bran, chocolate chips)

To cook, pour the contents of your sachet into a microwave-proof bowl, add ¾ cup of water and cook for 2–4 minutes (depending on your microwave).

Hints & Tips

✳ Grated apple is also a delicious flavouring, but is best grated fresh on the day.

Fruit yoghurt with toasted oats

Have you noticed how the yoghurt aisle has expanded to include loads of colourful containers with low-fat, high-sugar, fruit-flavoured options? Well forget about *all* them! Make your own full-fat yoghurt at home (page 97), or buy Greek-style yoghurt in big containers (it keeps for ages) and add your own favourite flavours. The toasted oats in this recipe make a great topping, as they keep you full for longer.

Serves 4

1 cup oats

¼ cup nuts, chopped

1 tablespoon butter melted with 1 tablespoon honey

pinch of cinnamon (optional)

2 cups plain Greek-style yoghurt

1 cup chopped fresh fruit (e.g. banana, mango) or berries

Preheat the oven to 160°C and line a baking tray with baking paper.

Place the oats and nuts in a small bowl with the melted honey and butter and the cinnamon (if using). Toss until well coated. Spread evenly over the prepared tray and bake for 10 minutes or until golden. Divide the yoghurt and fruit between four bowls and top each with a quarter of the toasted oats.

Cottage cheese and fruit lettuce wraps

This has got to be the easiest healthy breakfast ever.

Serves 4

4 large iceberg lettuce leaves

2 cups cottage cheese (see homemade recipe, page 101)

½ cup peanut butter

1 apple, grated

½ cup sultanas

1 banana, sliced

honey, for drizzling (optional)

Lay the lettuce leaves out like you would pieces of flat bread. Spread the cottage cheese over each leaf and top with a heaped tablespoon of peanut butter, a quarter of the apple, a tablespoon of sultanas, a quarter of the banana and a drizzle of honey (if using). Roll up the lettuce leaf and enjoy!

Banana and strawberry breakfast smoothie

Lots of people adore breakfast smoothies. They taste absolutely delicious made with Greek-style yoghurt, but feel free to use low-fat yoghurt if that's your thing.

Serves 1

1 ripe banana

½ cup rolled oats

¼ cup strawberries

⅓ cup milk (any kind)

1 cup plain unsweetened yoghurt

Place all the ingredients in a blender and blitz until well combined. Serve cold.

Toast three ways

Toast doesn't have to be boring, especially if you make your own bread. But even if you don't, you can be adventurous with your toppings. My personal favourite is peanut butter and banana. Here are a couple of old-fashioned options that you may have forgotten about.

EGGS ON TOAST

I always keep a few boiled eggs in the fridge for a quick breakfast. I like mine hard-boiled (I mark them with a big 'H' so they don't get them mistaken for raw eggs), but you can also make them soft-boiled. Eggs are great sliced on toast with a bit of Worcestershire sauce or added to a wrap or a salad for a protein hit.

Place some room-temperature eggs in a saucepan with plenty of cold water. Bring to the boil over medium heat. As soon as the water boils, take the pan off the heat, cover with a lid and set your timer.

— Soft boiled (runny yolks and cooked but soft whites): leave in the pan for 4 minutes.

— Squishy yolks and firm whites: leave in the pan for 6–8 minutes.

— Hard boiled (firm yolks and firm whites): leave for 10–12 minutes.

Drain and plunge the eggs into cold water. Store in the fridge in their shells for up to 1 week.

CINNAMON TOAST

An oldie but a goodie. Toast your bread as normal, spread it with butter, and top with a sprinkle of brown sugar and a pinch of cinnamon. Simply delicious!

FRENCH TOAST

To make this old favourite, grab two slices of any bread you fancy (though sourdough or wholegrain varieties are better for you). In a shallow bowl, beat 1 egg with 2 tablespoons of milk until well combined. Dip your bread into the mixture, first on one side and then on the other, until all of the mixture is soaked up. Heat a dob of butter in a small frying pan over medium heat until bubbling. Place your 'eggy bread' in the pan and cook for 1–2 minutes on each side, or until nicely browned. Serve with a drizzle of maple syrup if you have a sweet tooth, or a pinch of salt and pepper if your prefer it savoury.

Perfect scrambled eggs

I always make my scrambled eggs in the microwave because it's not only super fast (usually less than 2 minutes) but also makes them really fluffy and you don't need any butter.

Serves 4

4 eggs

¼ cup milk

salt and pepper

4 slices of bread, toasted

Crack the eggs into a microwave-proof container. Add the milk and whisk until well combined. Microwave on high for 30 second stints until the mixture starts to set on the sides. Scoop any curds that form around the edges back into the mixture then return to the microwave for 15 second stints until the mixture is just set. Serve on toast seasoned with a little salt and pepper. Perfection every single time!

Breakfast rice

When I was a kid, my mum would always cook more rice than was needed for our meals. She would then use the excess to make a delicious rice pudding for dessert (see the recipe on page 308) or this simple, yummy breakfast the next morning.

Serves 6

3 cups leftover cooked white or brown rice

1½ cups milk

1½ tablespoons butter or margarine

pinch of salt

pinch of cinnamon

Place all of the ingredients in a large saucepan over medium heat. Cook for 10–12 minutes, stirring frequently, until all of the milk is absorbed. The porridge will be hot and starting to go a little gluggy. Serve immediately.

Egg and bacon English muffins

This recipe is perfect for cooking in bulk and freezing so you can grab one on the go.

Serves 4 + 8 to freeze

12 English muffins, store-bought or homemade (see recipe page 94)

12 eggs

6 bacon rashers, halved

12 slices of cheese

⅓ cup barbecue or tomato sauce

oil, for greasing

Preheat the oven to 180°C. Grease a 12-cup muffin tray with vegetable oil.

To cook the bacon, heat a frying pan over medium heat. Add the bacon and cook for 5–6 minutes, or until crispy. Set aside to cool.

Crack an egg into each of the muffin cups and bake for 15 minutes or until just set.

Meanwhile, split the muffins and toast under the grill (or in batches in a four-slice toaster).

Remove the eggs from the oven and loosen with a spatula. To assemble the muffins, place a slice of cheese, a teaspoon of sauce, an egg and a piece of bacon on a muffin half and top with the other half. Serve hot.

Hints & Tips

＊ To freeze the leftover muffins, allow them to cool to room temperature. Wrap them individually in baking paper then plastic wrap and freeze for up to 3 months. To serve, allow to thaw for 10 minutes on the bench, then microwave on high for 1 minute or until heated through.

Baked pancake squares

This recipe can only be considered genuinely frugal if you have a friend or neighbour with chooks and you don't have to pay for all the eggs!

Serves 4–6

80 g (⅓ cup) butter

6 eggs

1 cup milk

1 cup plain flour

pinch of salt

1 teaspoon vanilla extract

icing sugar, for sprinkling

Preheat the oven to 180°C and line a 30 cm × 20 cm slice tin with baking paper.

Dob the butter evenly over the baking paper. Pop the tin in the oven for a couple of minutes to melt the butter. Remove from the oven.

Place the eggs, milk, flour, salt and vanilla in a food processor and process until the mixture is nice and smooth. Pour the batter into the baking dish on top of the melted butter and bake for 20 minutes or until golden and puffy. Cut into squares, sprinkle with icing sugar and eat while hot!

Amish buttermilk biscuits

Last year my parents visited Amish Country in the United States and came back with a gorgeous little handwritten recipe book from the area. It is something I truly treasure – the recipes are simple, frugal and really delicious. This is one of my favourites from the book. I should explain that although they're called biscuits, they're really more like scones.

Makes 10

3 cups self-raising flour

¾ teaspoon salt

⅓ cup softened butter

1 cup buttermilk (see tip below)

Preheat the oven to 190°C and line a baking tray with baking paper.

Sift the flour and salt into a bowl. Using your fingertips, rub the butter into the flour until the mixture is crumbly. Add the buttermilk and mix with a butter knife until the mixture is just combined (the dough will be a bit sticky). Turn the dough out onto a sheet of baking paper, cover with another sheet and roll out to a thickness of about 1.5 cm. Peel off the baking paper. Using a scone cutter, cut out 10 biscuits and place them on the prepared tray. Make sure you gather up any offcuts and form those into biscuits, too. Bake for 15 minutes or until golden. Serve warm with butter and jam. If you have any left over, you can freeze them in individual zip-lock bags for up to 3 months.

Hints & Tips

✳ If you don't have buttermilk, just add a teaspoon of vinegar to the milk and allow it to sit for about 10 minutes until it curdles.

Homemade pancake or waffle mix

Pancake mix is great to make in bulk. (I keep mine in the freezer to avoid moths – they just love it!) The great thing about this mixture is that it can also make waffles (if you have a waffle maker).

Makes 4 pancakes for every 2 cups of mix

MIX

6 cups plain flour

4 teaspoons baking powder

1 tablespoon salt

⅓ cup sugar

PANCAKES

2 eggs

1½ cups milk

¼ cup melted butter

2 cups homemade pancake mix

butter or canola oil, for cooking

In a large bowl, sift the flour, baking powder and salt together. Add the sugar and stir well. Pour into a larger container, seal and place in the pantry or freezer until needed.

To make the pancakes, place the eggs, milk and butter in a bowl and stir well to combine. Add 2 cups of the dry ingredients and whisk well.

Heat up a frying pan and lightly grease with butter or canola oil. Add as little or as much of the pancake mix as desired. Cook for 2–3 minutes on each side or until golden. Serve hot!

Hot potato breakfast fry-up

You just have to love the humble potato. So cheap, so versatile, so filling. Whenever you are cooking potatoes for dinner, always throw in a few extras so you can make a mouth-watering breakfast like this one! This works well with sweet potato, too.

Serves 2

2 tablespoons olive oil

1–2 cooked potatoes (about 250 g), diced

2 eggs

salt and pepper

In a small frying pan, heat up the oil until sizzling. Add the potato and cook until crispy all over (about 6 minutes).

Meanwhile, heat up a grill. When the potatoes are crisp, spread them evenly over the base of the pan and turn off the heat. Crack the eggs over the potatoes, season and place under the grill for 3–4 minutes or until the eggs are set. Enjoy!

Dairy- and egg-free sultana pancakes

These are truly cheap and easy to make. Feel free to use any dried fruit you like – dates, dried apricots, currants – they're all delicious!

Makes 6

1⅓ cups (200 g) self-raising flour

1 cup (160 g) sultanas

1 teaspoon sugar

pinch of salt

canola oil spray

Place all of the dry ingredients in a large bowl and mix until well combined. Add ½ cup of water and whisk to make a thick batter, adding a little more water if needed.

Heat a frying pan over medium heat and spray with some canola oil to prevent sticking. Drop about ⅓ cup of the batter into the pan and cook for 3–4 minutes or until bubbles appear on top. Flip and cook a further 2 minutes until golden on both sides. Repeat with the remaining mixture.

Hints & Tips

✳ For a gluten-free version, simply use gluten-free self-raising flour.

Banana and oat muffins

These are so delicious, I promise they'll become a staple at your house!

Makes 12

1½ cups plain flour

2 teaspoons baking powder

1 teaspoon bicarbonate of soda

½ teaspoon salt

1 cup rolled oats

½ cup white sugar

1 egg

¾ cup milk

⅓ cup melted butter

½ teaspoon vanilla extract

2 small overripe bananas, mashed

Preheat the oven to 190°C and grease a 12-cup muffin tray.

In a large bowl sift together the flour, baking powder, bicarb soda and salt. Add the rolled oats and sugar and mix well.

In another bowl, beat together the egg, milk, butter and vanilla. Add the mashed banana and mix well. Gently pour the wet ingredients into the dry ingredients and stir until just combined (do not over-mix). Spoon the mixture into the prepared muffin tray. Bake for 18 minutes or until a skewer inserted in the centre comes out clean. Allow to cool slightly before turning out onto wire racks.

Hints & Tips

✳ These will last in the fridge for 2 days.

Chicken noodle omelette

Serves 2

1 packet (about
70 g) chicken-flavoured
two-minute noodles

½ cup leftover chicken,
finely chopped

2 teaspoons dried parsley

½ cup grated cheddar

2 eggs, lightly beaten

1 teaspoon oil

Cook the noodles according to the packet
directions (including the flavour sachet) and
drain well.

In a bowl, place the noodles, chicken, parsley,
cheese and egg and mix well.

Heat the oil in a small frying pan over medium
heat. Pour in the mixture and cook for 5 minutes
(no stirring). Pop under the grill for a further
2 minutes to cook the top.

Corn fritters

I love corn fritters! They make a great breakfast, but they're also excellent as a snack or light lunch, or even as a side for dinner – gotta love a recipe like that! Plus they freeze really well.

Makes 8

2 corn cobs (or 1 × 310 g can sweetcorn kernels)

⅔ cup (100 g) self-raising flour

pinch of salt

1 tablespoon butter, melted

1 egg

¼ cup milk

canola oil spray

Using a sharp knife, cut the kernels off the corn cobs and set aside (or drain the canned kernels if using).

In a bowl combine the self-raising flour, salt, butter and egg. Add the milk and the corn to the mix and stir to create a thick batter.

Grease a large heavy-based frying pan with canola oil spray and place over medium heat. When hot, drop in dessertspoonfuls of the batter and cook for 3–4 minutes on each side until golden. Drain on paper towels and serve hot!

Cabbage pancakes

Now I'm not a big fan of cabbage, but I *love* these pancakes – so don't knock 'em until you try 'em! Chinese cabbage (napa cabbage, or wombok) is the crinkly, oval shaped light green cabbage that's sweeter and softer than other kinds.

Serves 4

2 eggs

3 cups (150 g) shredded Chinese cabbage

½ cup plain flour

1 cup milk

3 spring onions, thinly sliced (reserve a few for garnish)

1 tablespoon oil or butter

½ cup bean sprouts

1 long red chilli, finely sliced (optional)

In a large jug, whisk the eggs. Add the cabbage, flour, milk, half of the spring onion and ½ cup of water. Stir to make a thin batter.

Heat the oil or butter in a large frying pan over medium heat. Pour a quarter of the batter into the pan, spreading it evenly with a spoon. Cook for 2 minutes or until golden underneath. Flip and cook for a further 2 minutes. Transfer to a warm plate. Repeat with the remaining batter.

To serve, top with the bean sprouts, remaining spring onion and sliced chilli (if using).

Hints & Tips

* Use gluten-free flour and you've got another gluten-free recipe!

Hearty cauliflower breakfast waffles

Any type of pancake mix can easily be turned into waffles if you have a waffle iron. If you don't, they are not too expensive to buy new or you can usually find one second-hand online.

Serves 4

½ head of cauliflower (700 g), chopped into florets

2 cups breadcrumbs (see page 62)

salt and pepper

3 teaspoons dried herbs (optional)

2 eggs, beaten

1 cup grated cheddar

canola oil spray

Throw the cauliflower into a food processor and pulse until it resembles coarse breadcrumbs. (Be careful not to over-process, otherwise you'll end up with a puree!) Transfer the cauliflower to a large mixing bowl. Stir in the breadcrumbs, salt and pepper, herbs (if using), eggs and cheese. Mix well to combine.

Preheat your waffle iron and grease with canola oil spray.

Take ⅓ cup of the mix and place in the middle of the waffle iron. Close and cook until golden brown and crispy (about 6 minutes). Transfer to a plate and keep warm. Repeat with the remaining mixture. Serve hot.

Spaghetti omelette

I don't know about you, but every time I make spaghetti bolognaise
I end up cooking enough pasta to feed the whole neighbourhood! If this
sounds like you, don't chuck the excess spaghetti out – plonk it in the
fridge and make this yummy recipe the next morning.

Serves 2

2 teaspoons butter

2 cups cooked pasta (any
kind works for this recipe)

1 teaspoon crushed garlic

1 cup diced or chopped
vegetables (pumpkin,
sweet potato, broccoli,
etc.)

4 large eggs

1 cup grated cheddar

salt and pepper

In a large frying pan, melt the butter over
medium heat and add the cooked pasta.
Cook for about 5 minutes. Add the garlic
and vegetables and continue to cook, stirring
frequently, until the vegetables are soft and
the spaghetti is starting to brown.

In a bowl whisk the eggs and cheese and season
to taste. Pour the egg mixture evenly over the
pasta and cook for 2–3 minutes. Carefully flip the
omelette and cook for a further 1–2 minutes, or
until golden. If it looks like your omelette won't
hold together if you try to flip it, place the pan
under a grill to brown the top. Serve immediately.

Slow-cooker breakfast omelette

This recipe is perfect for the early riser, and a great way to use up stale bread. The slow cooker is truly my best friend in the kitchen! This omelette can also be cooked in the oven in a casserole dish, however the slow cooker almost 'steams' the food, giving it a glorious texture and taste.

Serves 4

4 slices of slightly stale bread, cut into triangles

2 teaspoons butter

5 eggs

½ cup milk

1 tomato, finely diced

½ cup diced ham, bacon or any leftover meat

½ cup grated cheddar

Set the slow cooker to high and cut a piece of baking paper to fit the base of the insert (this helps you remove the omelette in one piece!).

Butter the bread and place it butter side down on the baking paper, arranging the slices to minimise any gaps.

In a bowl, beat together the eggs and milk. Pour the egg mixture over the bread then top with even layers of tomato, ham and cheese.

Place the lid on the slow cooker and cook for 90 minutes or until the eggs are set. Remove carefully, cut into slices and enjoy!

Hints & Tips

✳ To make this in the oven, use a baking dish instead of the slow cooker, and follow the directions above, covering the dish with a lid (or foil) and cooking at 160°C for 12 minutes, or until the eggs are set.

Homemade hash browns

My two boys are mad keen on hash browns, but the shop-bought ones are always so greasy and expensive. These homemade versions are not only much tastier, but also surprisingly easy to whip up. Have them for breakfast, or serve with a salad for lunch. They make a great side for sausages!

Makes about 8

3 large potatoes (about 800 g), washed and grated

3 eggs, lightly beaten

1 teaspoon crushed garlic

1 teaspoon mixed dried herbs (optional)

canola oil spray

Wrap the grated potato in a clean tea towel and give it a good squeeze to remove as much liquid as possible. Transfer to a large bowl with the remaining ingredients and mix well. Leave to rest for 5 minutes.

Grease a frying pan liberally with canola oil spray and place over medium heat. When the pan is hot, drop 4–5 tablespoonsful of the mixture into the pan and press with a spatula. Cook until brown and crispy (about 4 minutes each side) and transfer to paper towel. Repeat with the remaining mixture. Serve immediately.

Three-ingredient banana pancakes

I love this recipe as it contains no dairy, gluten or sugar and takes about 10 minutes from start to finish!

Serves 2

2 eggs

1 teaspoon baking powder

3 very ripe bananas, mashed

canola oil spray

In a bowl, whisk together the eggs and baking powder until well combined. Add the mashed banana and mix well.

Grease a frying pan with a little canola oil spray and place over medium heat. When hot, add a quarter of the pancake mixture and cook for 3 minutes on each side or until golden. Transfer to a warm plate. Repeat with the remaining mixture. Serve immediately.

Baked bean crumpets

This is an easy breakfast, though I quite often make these for lunch.
I pick up crumpets when they are on sale and freeze them immediately.
They come in handy when I'm too flat out to make my own (see recipe
page 95).

Serves 4

8 crumpets

1 × 220 g can baked beans

½ cup grated cheese

Toast the crumpets (a four-slice toaster is always
handy!) Place a tablespoon of baked beans on
each crumpet and top with cheese.

Place under the grill and heat until golden and
bubbly. Serve immediately.

Hints & Tips

✳ This recipe works equally well using English muffins. Simply split four muffins and
toast the bottoms under the grill. Turn them over, top with beans and cheese and
grill until golden.

✳ This is also delicious with homemade baked beans if you have a little extra time
(see recipe page 138).

Oat and banana energy balls

These energy balls are super quick to make, free of processed sugar, and are great to eat on the run!

Makes 8 large or 12 small

1 cup rolled oats

2 very ripe bananas

½ cup sultanas

Preheat the oven to 160°C and line a baking tray with baking paper.

In a large bowl, mash the bananas thoroughly. Add the rolled oats and sultanas and mix well.

Roll heaped teaspoonsful of the mixture into balls and arrange on the baking tray. Bake for 15 minutes or until golden. Allow them to cool on the tray before moving to a cooling rack. These will last for 4 days in a sealed container in the fridge.

Homemade baked beans

These homemade beans are not only nutritious, but also taste awesome, especially served on toast with an egg or piled in a baked potato with a dollop of sour cream.

Serves 4

2 tablespoons olive oil

½ onion, diced

2 teaspoons crushed garlic

1 × 400 g can crushed tomatoes

2 teaspoons brown sugar

1 teaspoon vinegar

1 × 400 g can cannellini beans, drained and rinsed

salt and pepper

Heat the oil in a heavy-based frying pan over a medium heat. Add the onion and garlic and sauté for 2–3 minutes or until soft and golden.

Add the tomatoes, sugar, vinegar and beans and bring to the boil. Reduce heat, cover and simmer for 15 minutes.

Remove the lid and simmer for another 10–15 minutes or until the sauce has thickened enough to your liking. Season to taste.

Hints & Tips

✳ Store any leftovers in the fridge in an airtight plastic container and you can reheat them for easy meals for 3–4 days.

Lunches and savoury snacks

When it comes to lunches, reheating leftovers
or soup has to be the easiest way to go, and there
are heaps of delicious recipes later in the book where
you can do just that. In this chapter, I've included lots
of recipes that are great for school lunchboxes or as
snacks for growing kids, but I haven't forgotten busy
mums and dads – there are simple, healthy
recipes for us, too.

Toasted cheesies

I'm sure *everyone* has had one of these bad boys at some stage. They were a rite of passage while I was growing up, and I still have one now and again when I don't feel like cooking. They're perfect for an after-school snack.

Serves 1

1 slice of bread

1 tablespoon tomato or barbecue sauce

¼ cup grated cheddar

Heat a grill to medium and toast one side of the bread very lightly. Remove from the grill. Spread the sauce over the untoasted side of the bread and add the cheese. Pop back under the grill until the cheese is bubbling and almost starting to brown. Cut in half and enjoy with a glass of milk.

Easy cheesy muffins

This has got to be one of the easiest recipes I know. Plus, you can throw anything you like into the mix if you want some extra flavour (see tip below). Mixed herbs are great, but I love adding a pinch or two of chilli powder for some real zing!

Makes 12

2 cups self-raising flour

2 cups grated cheddar

2 cups milk or 1½ cups milk and ½ cup extra ingredients (see below)

butter, for greasing

Preheat the oven to 180°C and grease a 12-cup muffin tray.

Place all of the ingredients in a large bowl and mix well. Spoon evenly into the prepared muffin tray and bake for 30 minutes or until a skewer inserted in the centre comes out clean.

Hints & Tips

✳ You can add diced ham, chicken, tomato, capsicum, olives, mushrooms or pineapple, grated carrot, creamed corn, sliced spring onions or even a packet of French onion soup mix!

Sweet potato and ham croquettes

These delicious little morsels are a great way to use leftover sweet potato mash and are perfect for popping into school lunchboxes.

Makes 8

1 tablespoon butter

1 small onion, diced

1½ cups Sweet Potato Mash (see recipe below)

1 egg yolk

1 tablespoon milk or cream

½ cup diced ham

salt and pepper

1 cup plain flour

1 cup breadcrumbs

2 eggs

oil, for frying

In a large frying pan melt the butter over medium heat. Fry the onion for 5 minutes or until softened, but not browned. Transfer to a large mixing bowl. Add the sweet potato mash, egg yolk, milk or cream and ham, and stir well to combine. Season to taste. Cover the potato mixture with plastic wrap and refrigerate for several hours.

Sift the flour onto one plate, and pour the breadcrumbs onto another. Beat the eggs in a shallow bowl.

Roll tablespoonsful of the potato mixture into balls, coating them first in the flour (shaking off the excess), then dipping them into the egg mixture and finally rolling in the breadcrumbs.

Add enough oil to a frying pan to cover the balls and heat until hot. Fry the croquettes for 2–3 minutes on each side or until golden. Drain on a paper towel and enjoy!

Hints & Tips

✳ To make **Sweet Potato Mash**, Scrub and quarter 1 large sweet potato (about 400 g), cover with water and boil for 12 minutes or until soft. Mash with 1 teaspoon of butter and 2 tablespoons of milk. This makes about 1½ cups. (To make enough mash to serve four as a side, double the ingredients.)

Baked zucchini fries

These fries are a great way to use up zucchini, especially if you have them growing in the garden like I do! They make a great side dish and are a healthy snack for kids, too.

Serves 4

¾ cup breadcrumbs

¼ cup finely grated parmesan

1 teaspoon dried parsley

2 large eggs

3 zucchini, cut into finger-length batons

Preheat the oven to 240°C and line a baking tray with baking paper.

Place the breadcrumbs, parmesan and parsley in a small bowl and stir well to combine.

Crack the eggs into a second bowl and whisk lightly.

One by one, dip the zucchini sticks in the egg mixture and then roll in the breadcrumbs. Place in a single layer on the prepared tray. Bake for 12–15 minutes or until the zucchini is just tender and the coating is crispy and brown. Serve immediately.

Gluten-free potato cakes

Another great recipe using leftover potatoes! Serve these with Leafy Green Salad (see page 212) or top them with Homemade Baked Beans (see page 138).

Makes 8

2 cups (500 g) day-old mashed potato

¼ cup grated cheese (any sort)

1 tablespoon cream cheese

1 teaspoon crushed garlic

2 tablespoons milk

salt and pepper

2 tablespoons gluten-free flour

oil, for frying

Place the potato, grated cheese, cream cheese, garlic and milk in a large bowl and mix well. Season to taste. Add the flour sparingly until a dough is formed. (You may not need to use all of the flour, depending on the moisture content of the mashed potato.) Divide the mixture into eight balls then form each into a patty about 6 cm wide and 1 cm thick.

Heat about 2 tablespoons of oil in a frying pan over medium heat. When hot, cook the patties in batches for 4 minutes on each side or until golden. Serve immediately.

Spaghetti scones

A reader sent in this recipe, and I wasn't convinced about the flavour until I finally tried it myself. It's quite tasty and a hit with the little kids! Recipe by Cassie Billingsley.

Makes 12

1 cup self-raising flour

1 cup wholemeal self-raising flour

pinch each of salt and pepper

80 g (⅓ cup) butter, cut into small cubes

1 × 130 g can spaghetti in tomato sauce

1 tablespoon Worcestershire sauce

1 egg, lightly beaten

milk, for brushing

Preheat the oven to 190°C and line a baking tray with baking paper.

In a bowl, sift together the flours, salt and pepper. Add the butter and use your fingertips to rub it into the flour until the mixture resembles breadcrumbs. Add the spaghetti, Worcestershire sauce and egg and mix to a soft dough. Turn out onto a floured surface and knead until the dough just comes together – it will be pink!

Roll the dough out to a thickness of about 2 cm. Cut into rounds using a biscuit or scone cutter and place on the prepared tray. Brush the tops of the scones with milk and bake for 10 minutes or until lightly golden. Serve warm spread with butter.

Hints & Tips

✳ These scones are suitable to freeze for up to 2 weeks.

Easy sausage rolls

This is truly the easiest sausage roll recipe I've ever seen. Of course you can make it more interesting by cramming in some extra veggies, but if you wanted a three-ingredient version, here it is!

Makes 8

2 sheets puff pastry

1 egg, well beaten

500 g sausage mince

Preheat the oven to 190°C and line a baking tray with baking paper.

Place the puff pastry sheets side by side on a work surface. Beat the egg in a small bowl and place nearby with a pastry brush.

Place the sausage mince in a bowl and mix it with your hands until it is soft and pliable. Take half of the sausage meat and form it into a long 'log' shape along the centre of one of the sheets of puff pastry. Fold each side of the sheet pastry over the top, making sure the edges overlap slightly. Turn the sausage roll upside down and place it on one side of the prepared tray so that the seam is underneath. Brush with the egg. Repeat with the remaining meat and pastry. Cook the rolls for 25–30 minutes or until browned. Once cooked, cut each roll into 4 smaller rolls. Serve with tomato sauce.

Frugal bruschetta

A versatile snack that's delicious on its own, or can be served with soup for lunch or as an appetiser for dinner.

Serves 4

1 sourdough bread stick

2 teaspoons crushed garlic

¼ cup olive oil

3 large tomatoes, roughly chopped

1 red onion, diced

1 spring onion, sliced

1 tablespoon balsamic vinegar

Heat a grill to medium.

Cut the bread into 2 cm wide slices and arrange on a baking tray. Place under the grill for 3 minutes, or until very lightly toasted. Remove from the heat and turn over so the untoasted sides are facing up.

Mix the garlic and olive oil in a small bowl and lightly brush each bread slice. Place under the grill again and toast lightly for 2 minutes or until just beginning to colour. Remove from the heat and set aside.

In a small bowl, place the tomato, red onion, spring onion and enough of the vinegar to 'dampen' the mix. Top each piece of toast with a tablespoon of the tomato mix. Serve immediately.

Polenta chips

These are a delicious, healthy option for when you feel like something fancier than a potato mash. Serve with a salad for lunch, or as a fancy side with crumbed chicken.

Serves 4 as a snack or side

1 cup milk

1 cup polenta (cornmeal)

½ cup grated parmesan

salt and pepper

canola oil spray

Grease a 20 cm × 30 cm slice tin and line the bottom with baking paper.

In a large saucepan, mix the milk with 1½ cups of water and bring to the boil. Gradually add the polenta in a thin steady stream, whisking constantly. Reduce the heat to low and cook, stirring constantly with a wooden spoon, for 2 minutes or until the mixture is lovely and thick. Stir in the cheese.

Pour the mixture into the prepared tin and smooth it over. Set it aside on the bench to cool a little, then cover with plastic wrap and place in the fridge until firm (about 4 hours).

Preheat the oven to 200°C. Line another baking tray with baking paper.

When the polenta is firm, turn it out onto a clean bench or chopping board. Using a large knife, slice the slab into finger-length strips. Place the 'chips' on the baking tray (not touching each other) and spray liberally with canola oil spray.

Bake for approximately 30 minutes, turning halfway, until golden and cooked through. Sprinkle with a little salt and pepper and enjoy while hot.

Creamed corn and ham toasted wholemeal wraps

This is such an easy, delicious snack.

Serves 4

4 wholemeal or whole-grain wraps (or use my homemade tortillas, page 92)

1 × 310 g can creamed corn

8 slices of ham

4 slices of cheese

2 teaspoons butter

canola oil spray

Heat a sandwich press and spray lightly with canola oil.

Lay a wrap on a clean chopping board and place 1 heaped tablespoon of creamed corn in the centre. Top with one slice of ham, one slice of cheese and another slice of ham. Fold each side of the wrap over the filling to meet in the middle. Do the same with the top and bottom. (It should resemble an envelope.)

Spread ½ teaspoon of the butter over the wrap. Place it in the sandwich press and toast until hot and golden. Repeat with the remaining wraps and ingredients. Eat while hot.

Hints & Tips

* If you don't have a sandwich press, place the wraps in a 190°C oven or under a medium–hot grill for 5 minutes.

* Store the leftover creamed corn in a sealed container in the fridge for up to 4 days, or freeze it in a zip-lock bag for up to 3 months.

Cheese sandwich soufflé

Don't let the word 'soufflé' put you off! This is just a cute way to enjoy a hot cheese sandwich in a ramekin. And don't throw away the crusts, they make great breadcrumbs (see page 62).

Serves 1

3 slices of bread, crusts removed

¼ cup grated cheese

1 egg

2 tablespoons milk

salt and pepper

Preheat the oven to 200°C.

Place a slice of bread in a ramekin and spread over one-third of the cheese. Repeat with the remaining bread slices and cheese, finishing with a cheese layer.

In a separate bowl beat together the egg and milk. Season with a pinch of salt and pepper and pour over the top. Bake for 15 minutes or until golden and set. Enjoy with a spoon!

Mince scrolls

These are quite filling, so perfect for the school lunchbox.

Makes 12

1 tablespoon olive oil

1 onion, diced

1 teaspoon crushed garlic

300 g mince (beef, chicken, pork or turkey)

1 × 400 g can diced tomatoes

1 tablespoon tomato paste

2 tablespoons Worcestershire sauce

½ cup beef stock

2 cups self-raising flour

1 teaspoon white sugar

60 g (¼ cup) butter, cubed

¾ cup milk

1 cup grated cheese

Heat the olive oil in a frying pan over medium heat and fry the onion and garlic for 5–6 minutes or until soft. Add the mince and cook for 5 minutes or until browned. Add the tomatoes, tomato paste, Worcestershire sauce and stock and simmer for 25 minutes or until the mixture is nice and thick. Remove from the heat and allow to cool to room temperature.

Preheat the oven to 180°C and line a baking tray with baking paper.

Place the flour and sugar in a mixing bowl. Add the butter and rub it in with your fingertips until the mixture resembles breadcrumbs. Stir in the milk and mix to a sticky dough. Turn out onto a floured surface and knead for a couple of minutes until it just comes together. (It shouldn't be crumbly, but don't over-knead it so that it becomes stretchy.) Using a rolling pin, roll out the dough to a 40 cm × 30 cm rectangle.

Spread the mince mixture evenly over the dough and sprinkle with the cheese. With the long edge facing you, roll up the dough to make a sausage. Using a sharp knife, cut it into 12 even pieces. Place the scrolls on the prepared tray, allowing them a little room to spread. Bake for 25 minutes or until golden. Serve warm or cold.

Hints & Tips

✳ These freeze well, too. When cool, individually wrap in plastic (or use zip-locks if you prefer) and freeze for up to 2 months.

Tuna melts

Tuna melts are a super cheap and easy meal for when money is really tight. Enjoy them on their own, or as an accompaniment to soups or casseroles.

Serves 4

185 g tuna in spring water

1 small cucumber, peeled and finely diced

2 spring onions, finely diced

½ cup mayo
(see recipe page 80)

salt and pepper

1 French bread stick, cut into 1.5 cm slices

1 tomato, halved and finely sliced

½ cup grated cheese

Preheat the oven to 190°C and place the bread slices on a baking tray.

In a bowl, mix together the tuna, cucumber, spring onion and mayo. Season to taste with salt and pepper. Place teaspoons of the tuna mixture onto the bread slices then top with a slice of tomato and grated cheese. Bake for 10 minutes or until the cheese is melted. Enjoy while hot.

Cheesy beef puffs

This is a great way to use up leftover mince, plus anything with cheese is just plain *amazeballs*!

Makes 32

1 cup cooked minced beef (see recipe page 242)

½ cup cream cheese

½ cup grated cheddar

2 sheets puff pastry

milk for brushing (optional)

Preheat the oven to 200°C and line a baking tray with baking paper.

Place the mince, cream cheese and grated cheddar in a bowl and mix well.

Cut each sheet of pastry into 16 pieces (cut into quarters, then cut each quarter into quarters).

Place a teaspoon of mince mixture in the centre of each pastry square (don't overload). Fold over to form a triangle and seal the edges by pressing down with the tip of a fork. Brush with a little milk, if desired. Place on the baking tray and bake for 15–20 minutes or until golden.

Toad in the hole

Kids love this old-fashioned English dish, and it's a terrific way to use up cooked sausages after a barbecue.

Serves 4–6

1¾ cups (250 g) self-raising flour

½ teaspoon salt

2 eggs, beaten

2 cups (500 ml) milk

1 kg cooked sausages

½ cup breadcrumbs

salt and pepper

Preheat the oven to 180°C and grease a baking dish with a little oil.

Sift the flour and salt together and make a well in the centre. Add half of the egg and whisk in some of the flour from the edges of the well. Add the remaining egg and whisk again, taking a bit more flour. Gradually pour in the milk, whisking briskly between each addition, until all the milk has been added and a nice batter has been formed.

Cut the sausages into bite-sized pieces and arrange on the base of the baking dish. Pour the batter over the top. Sprinkle over the breadcrumbs and season with salt and pepper. Bake for 45 minutes or until the top is nice and golden. Serve with gravy and seasonal vegetables.

Savoury popcorn

I always have 'popping corn' kernels in the pantry, and have invested in a small popcorn maker (I got it on sale for $10) so the kids can make popcorn themselves. The good thing is that when you make it from scratch, it isn't full of fat and sugar.

Serves 4

1 tablespoon canola oil

¾ cup popping corn kernels

2 tablespoons vegetable stock powder

Heat the oil in a saucepan over medium heat. When hot, add the corn and place the lid on the saucepan. Give the pan a shake every 30 seconds or so (holding the lid). When the popping starts to die down, take it off the heat and transfer the hot popcorn to a bowl. Sprinkle the vegetable stock powder over the top and stir thoroughly.

Hints & Tips

✳ I like to use Vegeta stock powder, though Massel is also good – neither have MSG and are lower in salt than other stock powders (plus they are suitable for vegetarians and vegans).

Tuna salad on toast for one

This is another healthy option for busy mums. The kids might like it too – give it a go!

Serves 1

1 × 90 g can tuna, drained and flaked

1 tablespoon mayo (see page 80)

½ cup diced vegetables (celery, capsicum, spring onion, carrot)

1 teaspoon dried dill (or 1 tablespoon chopped fresh dill, if you have it)

2 slices of multigrain or sourdough bread, toasted

Place the tuna, mayo, veggies and dill in a small bowl and mix well. Spread over the toast – enjoy!

Salmon patties

I grew up eating salmon patties. We had them with veggies (or in a bread roll) for dinner, and then had them cold in our lunchboxes the next day. It is a great way to use up leftover mashed potatoes. Don't buy red salmon – that is wayyyy too expensive. The pink stuff will do just fine.

Makes 8

½ cup flour

1 × 440g can pink salmon, drained and flaked

2 cups mashed potato

1 cup breadcrumbs

½ cup grated cheese

3 spring onions, finely sliced

1 egg

2 tablespoons canola oil

Place the flour in a shallow bowl.

Combine the salmon, potato, breadcrumbs, cheese, spring onion and egg in a bowl and mix well. Divide the mixture into eight balls. Roll each ball in the flour then press between your palms to make a patty. Transfer to a plate, cover with plastic wrap and refrigerate for 30 minutes to firm up.

Heat the oil in a frying pan over medium heat. When hot, fry the patties in batches for 3–4 minutes on each side, or until golden all over. Drain on paper towel. Serve warm with a salad, veggies or make up your own salmon burgers. They're delicious with mayo and lettuce.

Baked bean nachos

This one is a firm favourite in our house, especially as an after-school snack, or even for dinner on Friday night when we're all tired. It can be thrown together in just minutes!

Serves 4

1 × 170 g packet plain corn chips

1 × 425 g can baked beans

1 cup grated cheddar

Preheat the oven to 180°C.

Spread the corn chips over the base of a large baking dish. Pour over the baked beans and top with the cheese. Bake until golden and crispy. Eat straight from the dish with the kids!

Hints & Tips

✳ You could also use homemade baked beans for this recipe (see page 138).

Paleo cauliflower flatbread

This gluten- and dairy-free flatbread makes a delicious accompaniment to soups and casseroles. It also makes an amazing pizza base.

Makes 2

½ head cauliflower (about 600 g), roughly chopped

2 large eggs, beaten

1 teaspoon curry powder

pinch of salt

Preheat the oven to 180°C and line two baking trays with baking paper.

Place the cauliflower in a microwave-proof container with a splash of water. Cook on high for 8 minutes, or until just tender. Drain well and allow to cool slightly. Transfer the cauli to a food processor and pulse until it resembles breadcrumbs (do not puree). Pour the blitzed cauliflower into a large bowl.

Add the beaten eggs and curry powder and mix thoroughly to form a 'dough'. Divide the dough in two equal portions. Place one half in the centre of one of the prepared trays, and press it out to make a circle. Use a rolling pin to get it as flat as possible without it breaking apart. Repeat with the remaining portion and place it on the other tray.

Bake for 15 minutes or until the 'flatbread' is firm enough to handle. Remove from the oven and allow to cool. Serve with soup, or roll up with any filling of your choice.

Vegetable and ham noodle muffins

All kids love instant noodles, which is great news for frugal parents as instant noodles are not only very cheap, but also easy to transform into a healthy lunchbox option.

Makes 12

2 packets (about 140 g) chicken-flavoured two-minute noodles

3 cups grated vegetables (e.g. zucchini, pumpkin, carrot)

2 eggs, lightly beaten

½ cup sour cream

½ cup diced bacon or ham

½ cup grated cheese

canola oil spray

Preheat the oven to 180°C. Lightly grease a 12-cup muffin tray with canola oil spray.

Cook the noodles as directed on the packet, reserving the flavour sachets. Drain the noodles, rinse under cold water to cool, drain again and place in a bowl. Add the chicken flavouring, vegetables, eggs, sour cream and bacon or ham. Stir until well combined. Spoon the mixture evenly into the muffin tray cups and top each with cheese. Bake for 30–35 minutes or until set. Best eaten the day they are made, hot or cold!

Hawaiian crackers

These are super easy to make and kids love them as an after-school snack. Get them to help you assemble the crackers – it's fun!

Makes 18

18 (about 60 g)
plain round crackers
(e.g. Ritz or Jatz)

2 tablespoons tomato
paste

½ cup diced ham

½ cup chopped pineapple

½ cup grated cheese

Preheat the oven to 200°C and line a baking tray with baking paper.

Arrange the crackers on the tray and spread each one with a little tomato paste. Sprinkle over the ham and pineapple then top with a pinch of grated cheese. Bake for 5 minutes or until the cheese melts. Serve immediately.

Cheesy Vegemite scrolls

This light scone mixture is the perfect vehicle for cheese and Vegemite. The scones freeze well for school lunches or just a yummy snack when you're on the go.

Makes 10

3 cups self-raising flour

½ teaspoon salt

50 g butter, cubed

1½ cups milk

1 tablespoon Vegemite

1½ cups grated cheddar

Preheat the oven to 220°C and line a baking tray with baking paper.

Sift the flour and salt into a large bowl. Using your fingertips, rub the butter into the flour until the mixture resembles fine breadcrumbs. Stir in 1 cup of the milk, mixing gently. Add as much of the remaining milk as you need to form a soft dough.

Turn the dough out onto a lightly floured work surface and knead for a couple of minutes until the dough comes together and is elastic. Use a floured rolling pin (or roll out between two sheets of baking paper) to make a 40 cm × 25 cm rectangle. Spread the Vegemite over the dough using a butter knife (or palette knife). Sprinkle three-quarters of the cheese evenly over the Vegemite.

With the long side facing you, roll up the dough into a log. Slice into ten pieces. Arrange the pieces cut side up on the prepared tray. Sprinkle the remaining cheese over the top. Bake in the oven for 15–20 minutes or until golden.

Hints & Tips

✳ To freeze, allow scrolls to cool. Individually wrap in plastic wrap and freeze for up to 2 months.

Puff pastry pizza pinwheels

These are great for kids' parties or a summer barbecue.

Makes 15

1 sheet puff pastry, thawed

2 tablespoons barbecue sauce

½ cup shaved ham or salami

¼ cup crushed pineapple, drained well

½ cup grated cheddar

1 egg, beaten

Preheat the oven to 190°C and line a large baking tray with baking paper.

Spread the sauce over the pastry. Evenly sprinkle over the ham, pineapple and cheese. Roll up the pastry quite firmly and cut into 2 cm 'rounds'.

Place on the prepared tray and brush the tops with the beaten egg. Bake for 10–15 minutes or until the pastry is puffed and golden. Enjoy hot or cold.

Muffin pizzas

I like to buy English muffins when they're on special and keep them in the freezer ready to make quick and easy meals and snacks. My boys love these little pizzas as an after-school snack.

Serves 2 for lunch or 4 as a snack

2 English muffins

2 tablespoons tomato or barbecue sauce

4 slices of ham

½ cup grated cheddar

Preheat the oven to 190°C or a grill to medium–high.

Separate each muffin and toast the halves lightly in the toaster, or place bottom side up on a tray and lightly toast under the grill.

Remove muffins from the toaster or grill. Spread 2 teaspoons of sauce over the inside of each muffin half then top with a slice of ham and a quarter of the cheese. Grill or bake the muffins for 4 minutes or until the cheese bubbles and just starts to brown. Serve hot.

Quiche in a cup

This is a really good way to use the crusty ends on a loaf of bread, and a great recipe for busy mums who rarely get something hot to eat!

Serves 1

1 egg

1½ tablespoons milk

salt and pepper

½ bread crust

2 teaspoons cream cheese, softened

2 tablespoons diced ham

Crack the egg into a microwave-proof cup. Add the milk and stir well with a fork. Season to taste with salt and pepper. Tear the crust into small pieces and add to the egg mixture along with the cream cheese and ham. Stir to combine.

Microwave on high for 1 minute then give it a stir and check if the egg is setting. Microwave for another 30 seconds or until set. Enjoy while hot!

Meatloaf in a mug

Yep, you read that right. It's a mini meatloaf. You'll need a large mug for this, or feel free to use a ramekin if you prefer.

Serves 1

1 slice of bread, finely diced

2 tablespoons milk

½ teaspoon tomato sauce

½ cup (125 g) minced beef

1 spring onion, finely sliced

salt and pepper

Place the bread in a large mug or ramekin with the milk and tomato sauce and leave to soak for 5 minutes, or until the bread has absorbed all of the liquid. Add the mince, spring onion and seasoning and mix well.

Microwave on high for 4 minutes, checking after 3 minutes, until the meatloaf is cooked through. Serve immediately.

Soups

Soups make the ultimate frugal meal,
as you can make them in big batches with cheaper
cuts of meat or bones and lots of veggies. They're
also easy to bulk up with croutons (page 90). Most of
the soups in this chapter will keep well in the fridge
in an airtight container for up to three days. They can
also be frozen. Just allow the soup to cool then ladle
individual serves into freezer-proof containers.
Soups made with meat can be frozen for up to
three months, while vegetable-based ones are
good for up to six months. Once thawed,
reheat them with a handful of fresh
vegetables to brighten them up.

Rustic tomato soup

Serves 4–6

2 kg ripe tomatoes, finely chopped

1 large onion, finely chopped

2 tablespoons sugar

salt, to taste

pinch of baking soda

2 tablespoons cornflour

½ cup milk

Place the tomatoes, onion, sugar, salt and ½ cup water in a large saucepan. Bring to the boil, then reduce heat and simmer for 1 hour.

Remove from the heat and strain mixture through a sieve, pressing with a spoon to extract all the juices. Discard the skins and seeds. Return the liquid to the pan and reheat. Add a pinch of baking soda.

Place the cornflour in a small jug and gradually add the milk, mixing until smooth and syrupy. Add to the soup before it comes to the boil and stir well to combine. Serve hot with Toasted Cheesies (page 140) or Easy Garlic Croutons (page 90).

Hints & Tips

✳ To freeze, allow soup to cool to room temperature. Pour 1 cup of soup into a zip-lock bag, seal, extracting as much air as possible, and lay flat (that way it takes up less room in the freezer). Freeze for up to 6 months.

Slow-cooker pea and ham soup

I adore this recipe – it's one I learned from Mum. However, as I'm the only one in my immediate family who likes it, I make a big batch in the slow cooker and freeze it in single-serve portions. Soaking the split peas overnight helps to reduce the 'fart factor', though if you don't have time, even soaking them while you prep the veggies will help.

Serves 8

500 g split peas
(yellow, green or
a mix), rinsed and
soaked overnight

1 ham hock (any size)

2 onions, chopped

2 carrots, diced

2 potatoes, diced

2 celery stalks, sliced

2 litres homemade
chicken stock
(see page 102)

Drain the split peas, discarding the soaking water, then give them a final rinse. Place them in your slow cooker along with the rest of the ingredients. Cook on high for 4 hours, stirring well after 2 hours.

When the peas start to go mushy and the liquid has reduced, the soup is ready. Transfer the ham hock to a bowl. Carefully remove the skin and fat and discard. Shred the meat using two forks and return it to the soup. Serve immediately with crusty bread.

Hints & Tips

＊ Ham hocks can be purchased from the deli section of your local supermarket. If you buy one from a butcher, make sure it's already cured and smoked.

＊ To make this meal even cheaper, use ham bones instead of ham hock, and use 3 stock cubes dissolved in 2 litres of water instead of homemade or store-bought liquid stock.

Emily's vegetable and lentil soup

This recipe is from my good friend Emily Rose who has written a variety of amazing cookbooks that I highly recommend. It appears here thanks to her generous nature.

Serves 4

1 onion, diced

2 medium carrots, diced

2 celery stalks, diced

1 potato, diced

1 × 400 g can crushed tomatoes

1 cup (200 g) red lentils

1.75 litres vegetable stock

salt and pepper

Place all ingredients in a large saucepan or stockpot and bring to the boil over a medium heat. Reduce heat, cover and simmer for 1 hour. Serve hot with Toasted Cheesies (page 140).

Sweet potato and pumpkin soup

Another delicious option for soup night, this one is also meat-free and therefore instantly frugal! You don't need to peel the sweet potato – you can just give it a good scrub.

Serves 4–6

800 g pumpkin, peeled, deseeded and chopped into 4 cm pieces

2 sweet potatoes, scrubbed and roughly chopped

1 onion, diced

1 teaspoon crushed garlic

1 cup orange juice

750 ml homemade chicken stock (see page 102)

1 rosemary sprig

Place all ingredients in a large saucepan or stockpot and bring to the boil. Reduce heat and simmer for 25 minutes or until the vegetables are very soft.

Remove the rosemary sprig and allow the soup to cool slightly. Transfer to a blender jug in batches (or use a stick blender in the pot) and blend until very smooth.

Reheat and serve with crusty bread and a dollop of sour cream or plain, Greek-style yoghurt.

Hints & Tips

✳ To make this even cheaper, use 3 chicken stock cubes dissolved in 3 cups of boiling water instead of the chicken stock.

Tomato, chickpea and chorizo soup

A big thankyou to Teresa Whitley for this delicious recipe!

Serves 4–6

1 teaspoon olive oil

2 chorizo sausages, diced (see tip below)

1 onion, diced

2 teaspoons crushed garlic

1 × 400 g can chopped tomatoes

1 × 400 g can chickpeas, drained and rinsed twice

1 litre vegetable stock

salt and pepper

Heat the oil in a heavy-based saucepan over medium–high heat until very hot. Fry the chorizo for 3–4 minutes or until it starts to become crisp. Remove the chorizo and set aside.

Add the onion and garlic to the pan and cook for 5 minutes, stirring, until soft. Return the chorizo to the pan and pour over the tomatoes. Cook for 10 minutes, uncovered, or until the mixture starts to thicken.

Add the chickpeas and vegetable stock, cover and simmer for 30 minutes. Season to taste with salt and pepper. Serve with Garlic Bread (page 59).

Hints & Tips

✳ Chorizo is a spicy, smoked and dried pork sausage available from the deli section of the supermarket. It needs to be cooked. If your budget doesn't stretch to chorizo, you can use salami.

Slow-cooker chicken and barley soup

A thick and hearty soup made with the deliciously nutty flavour and texture of barley.

Serves 6

750 g chicken thigh fillets

1 tablespoon olive oil

2 garlic cloves, crushed

2 onions, finely diced

5 carrots, diced

½ bunch celery (about 5 stalks), diced

2 zucchini, diced

2 litres chicken stock

1 cup (200 g) pearl barley

salt and pepper

Cut the chicken into bite-sized pieces, removing as much fat as possible.

Heat the oil in a frying pan over medium heat. When hot, fry the chicken in batches for about 5–6 minutes, or until browned on all sides. Remove from the pan and set aside.

Place the garlic, onion, carrot, celery and zucchini in the same pan and cook over medium heat until soft and starting to brown (about 5–8 minutes).

Transfer the chicken and vegetables to the slow cooker. Add the chicken stock and barley and mix well. Cover with the lid, and cook on high for 5 hours or until the barley is soft and the soup is lovely and thick. Season to taste and serve with Toasted Cheesies (page 140) or Garlic Bread (page 59).

Hints & Tips

✳ To make this recipe even cheaper, use chicken pieces such as drumsticks and wings instead of thigh fillets. Follow the recipe all the way until the soup is cooked, then simply remove the bones and any fatty skin (the meat will have fallen away from the bones).

Bacon and potato soup

Stay at Home Mum fans say this is one of their favourite recipes. It's a deliciously comforting soup, fit to warm your belly on a cold night. It also freezes very well, so make up a double batch!

Serves 6

2 tablespoons olive oil

4 bacon rashers, diced

1 teaspoon crushed garlic

1 leek, halved and finely sliced

750 g (about 6) potatoes, peeled and cut into 2.5 cm cubes

1 litre chicken stock

¼ cup cream

¼ cup chopped chives, to serve

salt and pepper

Heat the oil in a large saucepan or stockpot over medium–high heat. Add the bacon and cook for about 8 minutes, or until crispy. Remove from the pan with a slotted spoon and set aside.

Add the garlic and leek to the pan and cook for 3 minutes or until the leek is soft. Add the potatoes and toss to coat. Pour in the chicken stock, cover and bring to the boil. Reduce heat to low and simmer, partially covered, for about 20 minutes or until the potato is tender.

Use a stick blender to puree the soup in the pan (or transfer to a blender). Add the cream and ¾ of the cooked bacon.

Return the pan to low heat for about 8 minutes or until the soup is heated through. Season with salt and pepper. Serve hot topped with a sprinkle of chives, the remaining bacon and a side of crusty fresh bread.

Roast chicken and garlic soup

If you're unwell, forget chicken noodle soup – this is the one to try.
And, yes, there are *twenty* cloves of garlic in this soup – it's not a typo.

Serves 6

500 g chicken breast or
1 kg chicken pieces, skin
removed

2 tablespoons olive oil

2–3 garlic bulbs (about
20 decent-sized cloves)

1 onion, finely diced

2 teaspoons grated ginger

½ bunch celery
(about 5 stalks), finely
diced

2 carrots, finely diced

750 ml chicken stock

Preheat the oven to 180°C and line a baking tray
with baking paper.

Spread the chicken evenly over the tray and
drizzle with 1 tablespoon of the olive oil. Separate
the garlic bulbs into cloves, leaving the skins on,
and sprinkle around the chicken pieces. Bake
for 20 minutes or until the chicken is cooked
through and the garlic is baked and starting to
caramelise. Allow the chicken to cool slightly and
then either dice up the chicken breast, or peel the
meat from the chicken bones and set aside.

Gently squeeze the garlic cloves into a small bowl
until the cooked centres 'pop' out of their jackets.
Set aside.

In a large saucepan, heat the remaining
tablespoon of oil over medium heat. Add any
juices from the baking tray along with the onion,
ginger, celery and carrot. Fry for 5–6 minutes or
until the onion is starting to colour. Reduce the
heat to low, add the chicken stock and simmer for
10 minutes. Add the chicken and garlic and cook
for another 3–4 minutes, or until heated through.
Serve with crusty bread and salad.

Cream of pumpkin soup

Pumpkin soup is king when it comes to pleasing the whole family. Kids love its plain, smooth sweetness, while adults can enjoy it spiced up with a little Thai curry paste. You can make huge batches of this soup and freeze it in zip-lock bags for up to 6 months.

Serves 6

750 g peeled and deseeded pumpkin, cut into 4–5 cm chunks

1 onion, finely diced

½ teaspoon salt

2 cups milk (any kind)

2 teaspoons sugar (optional)

½ teaspoon nutmeg (optional), plus extra to serve

TO SERVE

sour cream

chopped fresh parsley

¾ cup Garlic Croutons (see page 90)

Place the pumpkin, onion and salt in a large saucepan. Pour in just enough water to cover (about 3–4 cups, depending on your pan). Cover and bring to the boil over medium heat. Reduce the heat to low and cook until the pumpkin is tender (about 20 minutes).

Transfer to a blender with the milk and puree until lovely and smooth. Return the puree to the saucepan. Add the sugar and nutmeg (if using). Cover and reheat over low heat for about 5 minutes. Serve with a dollop of sour cream, a sprinkle of parsley, a pinch of nutmeg and the croutons.

Hints & Tips

* To make Thai curry pumpkin soup, add 1 teaspoon of Thai curry paste instead of the nutmeg.

* When choosing pumpkin for your soup, pick the variety that you can afford and that has the brightest orange flesh (I like Jap/Kent pumpkin). Usually the brighter the colour, the sweeter the pumpkin.

'Lose a kilo' soup

I'm not a fan of diets or exercise, but I do love eating, and this lovely soup hits the spot when I feel like devouring a cream bun or a block of chocolate. I prefer my soup chunky, but feel free to blend yours if you prefer it smooth. If my pants are feeling tight, I make a batch!

Serves 4

1 teaspoon olive oil

1 large onion, diced

1 teaspoon crushed garlic

3 celery stalks, finely chopped

1 carrot, skin left on, trimmed and finely chopped

2 litres low-salt chicken stock or homemade stock (see page 102)

2 cups (150 g) shredded cabbage

1½ cups (150 g) broccoli florets

2 large handfuls of baby spinach leaves

1 cup brown lentils, soaked overnight and drained

salt and pepper

Heat the olive oil in a large saucepan or stockpot over medium heat. Add the onion, garlic, celery and carrot. Cover and cook for 10 minutes or until softened but not browned.

Add the chicken stock, cabbage, broccoli and spinach. Cover and bring to a simmer. Stir in the lentils and simmer for 25 minutes or until the lentils are tender. Season to taste. Serve hot.

Hints & Tips

✳ I always leave the skin on my carrots and potatoes where I can – that's where loads of the goodness is, and in soup you hardly notice it. Give it a go!

Slow-cooker beef and barley soup

There is nothing quite like a cold winter's day huddled inside with the slow cooker simmering away, especially when you know it's cooking this hearty and delicious soup. This one makes a meal on its own and is even tastier the next day!

Serves 6

1.5 kg gravy beef, cut into 1.5 cm cubes

1 cup pearl barley

2 onions, diced

1 green capsicum, roughly chopped

4 carrots, skin left on, trimmed and roughly chopped

1 × 400 g can diced tomatoes

1 tablespoon tomato paste

1 litre beef stock

Place all of the ingredients in the slow cooker and stir well. Cover and cook on low for 8 hours, stirring occasionally. If the mixture starts resembling a casserole rather than a soup, add more water. Serve with homemade bread rolls (page 91) or crusty fresh bread.

Leftovers and one-pan meals

This chapter is all about using up leftovers and making do. I adore leftovers because it means I have to spend less time to make another meal. Plus they are really versatile – leftover cooked meat can be turned into a pie, served with a baked potato or tossed in a salad. Leftover roast vegetables can be made into a delicious frittata or even served on a pizza! Most of the one-pan recipes in this chapter use small amounts of bacon or ham along with cheese, eggs and veggies to create super simple, super cheap meals.

The 'baked potato' buffet

This recipe is a beauty if you have extra kids for sleepovers. You simply provide a variety of ingredients and let everyone 'build' their own baked potato. The quantities in this recipe are just a rough guide – you may find yourself using more or less ingredients, depending on who's at the dinner table. Other options for your spud fillers include steamed broccoli (trust me – it's delicious with bacon and sour cream!) and leftover bolognaise sauce.

Serves 4–6

8 large brushed potatoes, washed well and dried

2 tablespoons olive oil

4 bacon rashers, diced

1 cup grated cheese

1 cup sour cream

1 cup Tomato Salsa (see below)

1 cup Quick Coleslaw (see below)

Preheat the oven to 200°C. Wrap each potato in aluminium foil and bake for 1 hour, or until soft when pierced with a skewer. Allow to cool slightly before serving.

Meanwhile, heat a frying pan over medium heat and cook the bacon for 4 minutes, or until crispy. Drain on paper towel and transfer to a bowl.

Place grated cheese, sour cream, salsa and broccoli in separate bowls in the centre of the table.

To serve, place the baked potatoes on a serving platter and let everyone help themselves. Younger children may need help opening the foil to avoid burning their fingers.

TOMATO SALSA

To make a simple salsa, mix together 1 cup chopped tomatoes with ¼ cup finely diced capsicum, 2 finely sliced spring onions and 1 tablespoon of sweet chilli sauce.

QUICK COLESLAW

To make a quick coleslaw, combine 1 cup of finely shredded cabbage, 1 cup of grated carrot, 2 tablespoons of mayo and 2 tablespoons of cream in a bowl and mix well. Season to taste with salt, pepper and a pinch of mustard powder (or whatever takes your fancy).

Depression era 'what ya got' casserole

I found this recipe in an old newspaper clipping that unfortunately wasn't dated, but the paper was really yellow, so it must have been old!

Serves 4–6

60 g butter

2 carrots, diced

1 onion, diced

3 celery stalks, diced

2 tablespoons plain flour

2 cups milk

1 cup stock

salt and pepper

1–2 cups cubed bacon, ham or any leftover meat

6 washed potatoes, skin left on, thinly sliced

Preheat the oven to 180°C. Grease a large casserole dish and set aside.

Melt the butter in a large saucepan over medium heat. When bubbling, add the carrot, onion and celery and cook until softened (about 5 minutes). Add the flour and cook, stirring continuously, for 1 minute. Add the milk and stock and continue stirring until the mixture is thick and soupy.

Season, add the meat and pour into the prepared casserole dish. Layer the potato slices over the top and bake for 40 minutes or until the potatoes are browned and crispy. Serve hot with a side of extra steamed vegetables.

Fried rice

This is such versatile dish – you can add just about anything to suit your family's tastes.

Serves 4

1 cup brown rice

4 bacon rashers, diced

1 onion, diced

1 cup mixed frozen vegetables

1 egg, beaten

2 tablespoons soy sauce

Place the rice in a saucepan with 2 cups of water. Cover and bring to the boil over medium–high heat. Reduce the heat to low and cook, covered, for about 10 minutes or until most of the water has been absorbed. Turn off the heat, leave the lid on and allow the rice to finish cooking for about 5 minutes.

Heat a frying pan over medium–high heat and fry the bacon and onion for 8–10 minutes or until the onions are soft and the bacon is starting to crisp. Reduce the heat to medium and add the frozen vegetables and ¼ cup of water. Cover and cook for 3–5 minutes, or until the vegetables are tender but still bright in colour.

Stir in the cooked rice, mixing well. Push the mixture to one side of the pan and pour egg directly onto pan (so it cooks like an omelette). Let it cook for 30 seconds then mix it in with the rest of the rice. Stir in the soy sauce and cook for 2–3 minutes or until the egg is fully cooked. Serve immediately.

Hints & Tips

✳ To make this dish even cheaper, omit the bacon or use any leftover meats you have from the night before – any meat works well!

Impossible pie

The title is ironic – this one is dead easy. You literally throw everything into a bowl, mix and then cook. It forms its own base, filling and top.

Serves 4

3 tablespoon butter

1 onion, diced

½ cup shredded ham

¾ cup plain flour

1 cup chopped mixed vegetables (frozen or fresh)

2 cups milk

4 eggs

½ cup grated cheddar

Preheat the oven to 180°C and grease a 24 cm pie dish.

Heat the butter in a small frying pan over medium heat. Add the onion and cook for 5–8 minutes or until soft and golden. Transfer to a large mixing bowl with everything except the cheese and stir until well combined. Pour into the pie dish and top with the cheese. Bake until golden and set (about 30 minutes). Cut into wedges and serve with Leafy Green Salad (page 212).

Zucchini slice

I adore zucchini. They are easy to grow at home, and when I have a glut of them, I make this slice. It freezes well, and makes for a great breakfast, lunch, dinner or snack. Plus, the kids love it. (I don't think they realise it contains so many healthy ingredients!)

Serves 4

1 tablespoon butter

1 onion, finely diced

1–2 bacon rashers, diced

400 g (3 or 4) zucchini

¾ cup self-raising flour

½ cup grated cheddar

4 eggs, lightly beaten

Preheat the oven to 180°C and grease a shallow casserole dish or quiche dish.

Melt the butter in a frying pan over medium heat and gently fry the onion and bacon until lightly browned (about 5–8 minutes). Remove from the heat and leave to cool.

Meanwhile, grate the zucchini into a large mixing bowl. Add the flour and mix well. Stir in the cooled onion and bacon mixture. Add the cheese and eggs and mix well. Pour into the prepared dish and bake for 30 minutes or until the top has browned and the eggs are set.

Hints & Tips

✳ To freeze, allow the slice to cool to room temperature then cut into squares. Wrap each square in plastic wrap and freeze for up to 2 months.

Impossible pizza

This super simple recipe is great for those nights when you can't be bothered slaving over a hot stove. It's ready in less than 30 minutes!

Serves 4

1 cup breadcrumbs
(see page 62)

4 eggs

1 cup milk

4 bacon rashers, diced

½ onion, diced

¼ cup finely diced
capsicum

1 cup grated cheddar

¼ cup (30 g) pitted black
olives, finely chopped
(optional)

Preheat the oven to 180°C and grease a large round pie dish or quiche dish.

Spread the breadcrumbs evenly over the base of the dish. In a mixing bowl, whisk the eggs and milk until well combined. Stir in the remaining ingredients. Slowly pour the egg mixture over the breadcrumbs.

Bake for 15–20 minutes or until golden brown and set. Cut into wedges and serve with Leafy Green Salad (page 212).

Hints & Tips

✳ Instead of bacon, you can use ham, salami, chopped chorizo or even leftover chicken – whatever you have on hand!

Savoury bread and butter pudding

Once you try this recipe I'm sure it will become just as popular at your house as it is at ours! This is a good one to cook just before shopping day to use up any bits and pieces in the fridge.

Serves 4–6

5 slices of multigrain bread

4 eggs

½ cup milk

100 g (½ punnet) cherry tomatoes, halved

½ cup diced ham or bacon

2 tablespoons chopped parsley

½ cup grated cheddar

Preheat the oven to 180°C. Grease a 20 cm × 20 cm casserole dish with a little butter.

Place four of the bread slices flat in the dish, cutting crusts to fit if necessary (reserve the crusts for the top).

Whisk the eggs and milk in a jug and pour over the bread base. Place the halved cherry tomatoes cut side down on the bread. Sprinkle over the ham or bacon and the parsley. Cut the last piece of bread (and any reserved crusts) into 5 mm cubes and scatter on top. Sprinkle over the grated cheese. Bake for 30 minutes or until the top is golden brown and the eggs are set. Serve hot or cold.

Hints & Tips

* To make a gluten-free version, simply use gluten-free bread.

* Keep leftovers in an airtight container in the fridge for up to 2 days, or in zip-lock bags in the freezer for up to 1 month.

Two-ingredient pizza base

If you want a quick, easy and super-healthy alternative to making your own pizza bases, try this version!

Makes 1 large pizza base

2½ cups self-raising flour, sifted

1 cup plain Greek-style yoghurt

Preheat the oven to 200°C. Line a large pizza tray with baking paper or aluminium foil.

Mix the two ingredients together in a bowl and then transfer to a floured surface and knead until smooth. Roll out to your desired thickness and transfer to the prepared tray. Now add any toppings you like, though remember that less is more when it comes to homemade pizza. Bake for 12 minutes or until the base is crusty and the toppings are cooked.

TOPPINGS

— chicken, sweet chilli sauce, pumpkin and cheese

— pumpkin, cheese and walnuts

— leftover roast vegetables, barbecue sauce and cheese

— basil pesto, cherry tomatoes and cheese

TV dinner

This is basically mince and vegetables cooked in a pocket of aluminium foil. Because they are all cooked together, the juices from the meat go into flavouring and cooking the vegetables. This is one version that our family loves, but you can use any ingredients you fancy.

Serves 1

1 uncooked hamburger patty or 3 meatballs

1 small potato, sliced

½ onion, sliced

1 cup sliced vegetables (carrots, zucchini, corn)

1 teaspoon butter

salt and pepper

Preheat the oven to 180°C.

Tear off about 60 cm of foil and fold it in half for extra strength (shiny side out). Place the meat in the middle of the square and arrange the vegetables around it. Add the butter and season to taste.

Take each corner of the foil and bring it together to meet in the centre, pressing to make an airtight parcel. Place in the oven and cook for 1 hour.

Hints & Tips

✴ This is a great recipe for camping – follow the method above and simply cook the parcels in your campfire coals.

Tuna and steamed vegetables for one

I quite often have this for lunch as it's warming, easy and very healthy!

Serves 1

1 × 90 g can flavoured tuna (see tip below)

1 × 200 g packet frozen vegetables

Cook the frozen vegetables according to the directions. While still piping hot, pour into a bowl. Pour the tuna over the top and mix through so that the flavour goes right through the vegetables. Enjoy!

Hints & Tips

✳ There are some great flavoured tunas available. These are my favourite flavours: Indian curry, puttanesca, sweet chilli, hot chilli, sun-dried tomato and basil.

Veal goulash

This is another great recipe from my good friend Emily Rose Brott. She feeds her four kids this meal regularly, and says that it is not only cheap but filling and that they always come back for seconds and thirds!

Serves 4

2 tablespoons olive oil

3 onions, halved and finely sliced

500 g veal on the bone

1 tablespoon sweet paprika

salt and pepper

Heat the oil in a saucepan over medium–high heat. Sauté the onions for 3–4 minutes or until soft and golden. Add the veal and cook for a few more minutes, moving the pieces around the pan to brown on all sides.

Add the paprika and season with salt and a little pepper and toss to coat. Turn heat to low and cook for 2 hours, stirring occasionally. If needed, add a small amount of water.

Serve with rice and veggies.

Corned beef fritters

Corned beef fritters are so damn yummy, and a great way to use up cooked corned beef from the night before. Actually, sometimes I only make corned beef so I can make the fritters! (I've included quick instructions for cooking corned beef below.)

Serves 4

150 g corned beef, finely diced

1 × 175 g can creamed corn

1 × 175 g can corn kernels

½ capsicum, finely diced

½ cup grated cheese

2 eggs

½ cup self-raising flour

salt and pepper

1 teaspoon mixed herbs (optional)

oil, for frying

Place the corned beef, creamed corn, corn kernels, capsicum, cheese and eggs in a large bowl and mix well. Gradually mix in the flour until the mixture becomes gooey but stays together. Add mixed herbs and season well.

Heat a little oil in a frying pan over medium–high heat. Working in batches, drop tablespoonsful of the mixture into the pan and fry for 3 minutes on each side until golden. Drain on paper towel. Serve with tomato sauce and a salad if you want to be healthy!

Hints & Tips

* To make **Slow-Cooker Corned Beef**, wash a 1.5 kg piece of corned beef or silverside and place in the slow cooker. Cover with water (the slow cooker should be about three-quarters full). Cook on high for 4 hours or low for 8 hours. Serve with white sauce and veggies, then use the leftovers to make a double batch of these fritters!

* To freeze your fritters, allow them to cool to room temperature and lay between sheets of baking paper in an airtight container. Label and place in the freezer for up to 3 months.

Slow-cooker sticky ribs

A lot of people are reluctant to buy ribs because they think they're too hard to cook, but this is truly so easy. Pick up some beef ribs when they're on special, though avoid pork ribs, as they can be incredibly fatty and it's tricky to drain off excess fat for this recipe.

Serves 4

2 kg beef ribs

1 cup barbecue sauce

Place the ribs in the slow cooker and pour over the barbecue sauce. Cook on low for 8 hours, stirring every so often. Serve on a big platter with a stack of paper towel and watch as everyone gets their faces covered in sauce!

Slow-cooker creamy garlic pot roast

I love a good pot roast – they're not only very cheap, but are very tasty. If you want to keep the vampires away, this is the perfect recipe for you. (You can never have too much garlic!)

Serves 4–6

1 tablespoon butter

2 tablespoons crushed garlic

2 medium onions, sliced into rings

1 kg pot roast (chuck or brisket)

250 ml cooking cream

1 × 40 g packet French onion soup mix

Set the slow cooker to high and allow it to heat up.

Place the butter, garlic, onion rings and meat in the slow cooker. Cover and cook for 30 minutes.

Combine the cream and French onion soup in a jug, stir well and pour over the meat. Reduce the heat to low and cook for 5 hours or until the meat starts to fall apart. Serve with crusty bread rolls, in a baked potato or with pasta.

Veggie dishes

Meat is expensive, so if you are serious about saving money, you'll need to have a few meat-free meals a week. But don't worry, you won't find boring recipes here! They're all tried and true by me and other Stay at Home Mums with meat-loving families.

Potato casserole

The starchy potatoes and creamy cheese make this is a bit of a naughty recipe (just because it's vegetarian doesn't mean it's healthy!), but if you can keep your portion size down and serve with Leafy Green Salad (page 212), it's absolutely delicious!

Serves 4

1 kg brushed potatoes (any variety good for mashing), peeled and halved

4 tablespoons butter

250 g cream cheese, room temperature

¼ cup milk

salt and pepper

1 spring onion, finely chopped

1 cup fresh breadcrumbs (see page 62)

canola oil spray

Preheat the oven to 180°C. Lightly grease a 20 cm × 20 cm casserole dish with canola oil spray.

Place the potatoes in a large saucepan, cover with water and bring to the boil over medium heat. Cook for 20 minutes or until very tender. Drain well and mash in the pan. Add 2 tablespoons of the butter, the cream cheese and the milk and mix well. Season to taste.

Pour the mixture into the prepared dish. Sprinkle over the spring onion and breadcrumbs. Top with dobs of the remaining butter. Bake for 30 minutes or until golden on top and heated through.

Tightwad mushroom risotto

Risotto is a good, filling meal that doesn't cost the earth. Stretch it (and amp up your nutrients) by serving it with a side of something green. I love steamed broccoli and zucchini, or a few lettuce leaves drizzled with a little olive oil and lemon juice.

Serves 4

1 tablespoon butter

1 onion, finely diced

1 cup sliced mushrooms (any sort)

1 litre vegetable stock

2 cups arborio rice

grated cheese or sour cream, to serve (optional)

Heat the butter in a large frying pan over medium heat. When sizzling, add the onion and mushrooms and cook for 5–6 minutes or until just starting to brown. Remove from the heat and transfer to a bowl.

Meanwhile, heat the vegetable stock in a jug in the microwave until almost boiling.

Return the pan to the heat (with an extra dob of butter if the pan is too dry). Add the rice and stir to coat, heating for 1–2 minutes or until the rice starts to colour. Pour in the vegetable stock 1 cup at a time and stir each addition until absorbed (about 5 minutes each). Add some water if you run out of stock. When the rice is cooked (it should take about 20 minutes), return the onion and mushroom mixture to the pan and stir to combine. Top with some grated cheese or sour cream if desired, and serve immediately.

Lentil curry

This works out to about 80 cents a serve – pretty cheap, right? And it just happens to taste delicious, too.

Serves 4

2 cups brown lentils, soaked overnight

1 tablespoon butter

1 teaspoon curry powder

1 teaspoon mustard seeds

1 teaspoon cumin seeds

1 onion, finely diced

1 teaspoon crushed garlic

1 × 400 g can diced tomatoes

Drain the lentils, rinse, and drain again.

Heat the butter in a large saucepan or stockpot over medium heat until bubbling. Add the curry powder and seeds and cook, stirring, for about 1 minute until fragrant. Add the onion and garlic and sauté for 5–6 minutes until soft.

Add the lentils, tomatoes and 1 cup of water. Bring to the boil, reduce heat, cover and simmer for 45 minutes or until the lentils are breaking apart and have thickened the stew. Serve with plain steamed rice.

Hints & Tips

✳ Add some cubed sweet potato with the tomatoes to make it stretch that bit further.

Veggie spaghetti pie

This is kind of like a quiche, but with spaghetti instead of pastry. It's an excellent way to use up any leftover cooked pasta you have in the fridge!

Serves 4

250 g spaghetti (or 3–4 cups leftover cooked pasta)

salt and pepper

1 cup steamed vegetables (broccoli florets, sliced zucchini, cubed pumpkin)

3 spring onions, finely chopped

2 tablespoons butter

6 eggs

½ cup milk

1 teaspoon herbs (basil, oregano, parsley or mixed)

½ cup grated cheese

Preheat the oven to 150°C and grease a 22–24 cm round pie dish with butter.

Cook the spaghetti (if using) according to the packet directions and drain well. Spread the cooked spaghetti or pasta evenly in the base of the pie dish. Top with the cooked vegetables and the spring onions.

In a large bowl, whisk together the eggs and milk and season to taste with salt and pepper. Stir in the herbs then pour it over the pasta and vegetables. Sprinkle with the grated cheese. Bake for 25 minutes or until the top is golden and the eggs are set. Serve sliced with Leafy Green Salad (page 212).

Three-ingredient quiche

This simple quiche is absolutely delicious alone, or with any extra ingredients you fancy. I love to add a little steamed broccoli, though feel free to throw in some sliced spring onion, cherry tomatoes or mushrooms, or some baby spinach, corn kernels, diced capsicum, or even some leftover roast pumpkin or spud!

Serves 4

3 eggs

1 cup sour cream

1 sheet of puff pastry

1½ cups finely chopped veggies (optional; see above)

½ cup grated cheese (optional)

Preheat the oven 180°C and grease a 24 cm quiche dish.

Line the base and sides of the quiche dish with the pastry, cutting off any excess and pressing it around the sides to fill in any gaps.

Whisk the eggs and sour cream together until smooth and season to taste. Add any extra ingredients you wish, and pour into the pastry shell. Bake for 30–35 minutes or until golden and set. Serve with a garden salad and crusty bread.

Stuffed sweet potatoes

What can I say – this is one of my *favourite* recipes!

Serves 4

4 sweet potatoes, scrubbed

2 tablespoons chilli oil (see tip below)

1 × 400 g can cannellini beans, drained and rinsed

1 cup grated cheese

chopped parsley, to serve

Preheat the oven to 180°C.

Place the sweet potatoes on a baking tray and lightly rub with chilli oil. Bake for 1 hour or until soft and cooked through.

Remove from the oven. Cut the top off each potato lengthways, scoop out a couple of spoons of the cooked flesh and place the tops and flesh in a bowl. Gently mash with a fork. Season to taste and stir in the beans. Spoon the bean filling evenly into each potato and top with the cheese and parsley. Bake for 15 minutes or until the cheese is melted and starting to brown.

✳ If you don't have any chilli oil, simply add a pinch of chilli to 2 tablespoons of olive oil and stir well.

Rice pilaf

This makes a tasty vegetarian meal on its own, though you can also serve it as a side.

Serves 2 as a main and 4 as a side

1 tablespoon olive oil

1 onion, diced

1 teaspoon cumin seeds

1 teaspoon caraway seeds

½ teaspoon ground turmeric

1 cup basmati rice

2 cups chicken stock

1 cup frozen vegetables

2 tablespoons currants

⅓ cup flaked almonds (optional)

In a heavy-based saucepan or deep frying pan, heat the olive oil over medium heat until hot and starting to bubble. Add the onion, cumin seeds, caraway seeds and turmeric. Cook for 3–4 minutes, stirring frequently, until the onion is soft and the spices fragrant. Add the rice and stir to coat. Pour in the stock, stir well, cover and cook for about 15 minutes, or until all the water is absorbed and the rice is just tender.

About 5 minutes before the rice is ready, stir in the frozen vegetables and allow to cook in the hot rice mixture. When the rice and vegetables are cooked, stir through the currants. Serve piled high with the sliced almonds on top.

Stuffed capsicums

Stuffed capsicums make a great meal in themselves or a very filling side.

Serves 4

3 cups brown rice

4 capsicums (any colour)

1 tablespoon olive oil

1 onion, finely diced

1 teaspoon crushed garlic

3 ripe tomatoes, diced

1 teaspoon curry powder

2 tablespoons slivered almonds (optional)

¼ cup fresh parsley leaves, finely chopped

¾ cup grated cheese

Preheat the oven to 180°C. Line a shallow baking tray with baking paper.

Place the rice in a saucepan with 6 cups of water. Cover, bring to the boil, reduce heat and simmer for 20–25 minutes or until most of the water has been absorbed. Remove from heat and leave to steam for another 10 minutes with the lid on.

Meanwhile, cut the tops off the capsicums and remove the seeds and pith. Place the capsicums cut side up on the baking tray and set aside.

In a frying pan, heat the olive oil over medium heat and fry off the onion and garlic until soft and fragrant (5–6 minutes). Stir in the curry powder and tomato and cook for 5 minutes or until the mixture is reduced and thickened. Stir through the steamed rice, add almonds and parsley. Spoon the mixture into the capsicums (not too firmly) and top with the grated cheese. Bake for 15–20 minutes or until the top is golden and bubbling. Serve immediately.

White bean risotto

Serves 4

¼ cup olive oil

1 onion, finely diced

1 teaspoon crushed garlic

3 cups chicken stock

2 cups arborio rice

1 × 440g can cannellini beans, drained

½ cup finely grated parmesan

salt and pepper

In a large frying pan, heat the oil over medium heat. When hot, add the onion and garlic and cook until soft and fragrant (about 5 minutes).

Pour the stock into a microwave-proof jug and microwave on high for 3–4 minutes or until nearly boiling.

Add the rice to the pan and stir until it starts to colour and is well coated in the onion mixture. Add 1 cup of the hot stock and stir constantly until absorbed. Continue adding the stock in this way, stirring constantly, until the rice is cooked (about 20 minutes). If the stock cools down, pop it back in the microwave for 30 seconds. Stir through the beans and parmesan and season to taste. When the beans are hot and the parmesan is melted, serve immediately.

Hints & Tips

* For a bit more colour and flavour, add ½ cup chopped fresh parsley with the parmesan.

Homemade gnocchi

I must admit that although I've made gnocchi quite a few times now, I always cut them a bit too large and they end up looking more like little potato cakes – but they are still delicious! I like them plain, fried in a little garlic and butter, though you can have them with any of the pasta sauces on pages 218–230.

Serves 4

1.4 kg (4 large) potatoes (floury ones good for mashing, not waxy ones)

pinch of salt

1 egg yolk

1¼ cups plain flour

Peel the potatoes and cut into quarters. Place in a large saucepan of salted water. Bring to the boil and cook for 25 minutes or until very tender. Drain and place in a bowl to cool a little. Mash them until they are almost lump free. Stir in the egg yolk and flour and mix to a rough dough.

Turn out onto a well-floured surface and knead briefly until the dough is just smooth (don't over-knead). Roll into a long 2 cm wide log and cut into 2 cm lengths. Roll each little piece into a ball and press down slightly with a fork. Set aside on a plate.

Refill the large saucepan with salted water and bring to the boil. Add the gnocchi 1 cup at a time – don't crowd the water – and cook for 2–3 minutes or until they float. Remove and drain on a paper towel. Serve with burnt butter, sage and parsley sauce, or any sauce that takes your fancy.

Potato omelette

If you can get your eggs cheaply, this will fill you up for just a few cents.

Serves 4

1 tablespoon butter

1 onion, finely diced

6 eggs, beaten

2 large potatoes (any kind), finely sliced

salt and pepper

Melt the butter in a large frying pan over medium heat. Add the onion and cook for 5–6 minutes until soft and golden. Add the potato slices along with a few tablespoons of water. Season well.

Cover and cook for 5–6 minutes or until soft, carefully shifting the slices around to prevent them sticking but without breaking them up.

When the potato is cooked, reduce heat to low and pour over the eggs. Cook for a 2–3 minutes or until the bottom is just starting to set.

Heat a grill to medium. Place the pan under the grill and cook for 3–4 minutes or until the eggs are set and the top is starting to brown. Cut into wedges and serve with crusty bread.

Gnocchi with burnt butter, parsley and sage

This is one of those simple recipes that is delicious enough to serve to guests. The gnocchi takes about an hour, but the sauce itself takes 5 minutes. So good!

Serves 4

1 batch homemade gnocchi (page 205)

80 g (⅓ cup) butter

½ cup sage leaves, roughly chopped (use the tender, small leaves)

½ cup pine nuts (optional)

½ cup fresh parsley leaves, finely chopped

Melt the butter in a frying pan over medium heat until it starts to bubble and froth and becomes a lovely golden colour (not dark brown!). Reduce heat to low. Add the sage and pine nuts and cook for 2–3 minutes until fragrant. Remove from the heat and stir through the parsley. Add the cooked gnocchi and stir to coat. Serve immediately.

Vodka risotto

Ah, yes. You read that right. Vodka. Now, don't go and buy a bottle just to make this (although you're welcome to do so if you can afford it), but if you have a bottle lying around, you'd be surprised at just how lovely this dish is. Obviously, this is not one for the kiddies.

Serves 4

60 g (¼ cup) butter

1 white onion, very finely diced

2 celery stalks, very finely diced

3 teaspoons crushed garlic

1½ cups arborio rice

2 litres vegetable stock

½ cup lemon juice

5 tablespoons vodka

⅓ cup grated cheese

salt and pepper

In a large heavy-based saucepan, heat the butter over medium heat. When sizzling, add the onion, celery and garlic and cook for 5–6 minutes or until the onion is translucent and the celery has softened. Add the rice and cook, stirring constantly, for 3–4 minutes or until the rice is well coated in the butter mixture.

Place the vegetable stock in a microwave-proof jug and microwave on high until almost boiling. (Or heat it in a saucepan on the stove if you prefer.)

Add the stock to the rice mixture, cup by cup, stirring constantly until each cup is absorbed. When the rice is nearly cooked, add the lemon juice and vodka, and season to taste. Heap into four bowls and top with the grated cheese.

Hints & Tips

∗ Store any leftover risotto in the fridge for up to 2 days. For best results, reheat on the stovetop with a little more water or stock.

Spinach slice

This recipe is even more delicious served cold the next day – awesome for lunchboxes, and so nutritious, too.

Serves 4

1 bunch spinach (about 400 g), washed, trimmed and roughly chopped

1¼ cups (250 g) cottage cheese

2 cups grated cheddar

3 eggs

1 tablespoon tomato paste

salt and pepper

Preheat the oven to 190°C. Line the base and sides of a 20 cm × 30 cm slice tin with baking paper or aluminium foil.

Place the spinach (it should still be wet after washing) in a microwave-proof bowl, cover and cook for 2 minutes or until wilted. Drain over a sieve.

In a bowl, whisk together the cottage cheese, cheddar, eggs and tomato paste. Season to taste. Stir through the cooked spinach. Pour into the prepared tin and bake for 35 minutes or until the top is lightly browned and the filling is set. Slice and serve with a salad or side dish of your choice.

Hints & Tips

✳ If you're out of tomato paste, tomato sauce or even barbecue sauce work well, too.

Smashed garlic potatoes

I found this recipe online years and years ago. It's such a simple concept, yet a great way to serve potatoes – they end up like big, crispy chips with fluffy insides.

Serves 4 as a side

8 small potatoes (about 1 kg), skin on, washed

60 g butter, melted

1 tablespoon crushed garlic

Preheat the oven to 200°C. Line a baking tray with baking paper.

Prick the potatoes and place in a microwave-proof container with a little water. Microwave on high for 10–15 minutes or until soft and cooked through.

Place the cooked potatoes on the prepared tray and, using a potato masher, crush each one gently until the middle spills out and it's about 1 cm high.

Combine the melted butter and crushed garlic in small jug and pour evenly over the crushed potatoes. Bake for 20 minutes or until crispy. These are delicious with Slow-cooker Creamy Garlic Pot Roast (page 193).

Rosemary potatoes

This is a delicious side for any meat dish. Try it with Slow-cooker Roast Chicken (page 261) or Traditional Aussie Rissoles (page 244).

Serves 4 as a side

1 kg floury potatoes (e.g. brushed or sebago) cut into 1.5 cm cubes

⅓ cup olive oil

3 teaspoons crushed garlic

3 sprigs rosemary, leaves picked (or 1 teaspoon dried rosemary)

salt and pepper

Preheat the oven to 200°C and line a baking tray with baking paper.

Place the potatoes in a bowl, cover with water and leave to soak for about 15 minutes.

Meanwhile, place the olive oil, garlic and rosemary leaves in a small jug and stir well.

Drain the potatoes and pat dry with paper towel. Spread them over the prepared tray and pour over the olive oil mixture. Cook for 35–40 minutes or until crisp and golden. Shake the pan a few times during cooking so the oil coats the potatoes well. Season with salt and pepper to serve.

Leafy green salad

Kids tend to prefer iceberg lettuce because of its subtle flavour and crunch, but I like to mix it up a bit and use cos lettuce, baby spinach, or whatever I have in the garden. Avocado is a delicious addition if it's in season (and cheap). You can also toss through a few diced leftover roast veggies – pumpkin and sweet potato are especially tasty.

Serves 4 as a side

4 large iceberg lettuce leaves, torn (or 2 large handfuls of any other lettuce)

2 handfuls of baby spinach

1 handful of cherry tomatoes, halved

½ Lebanese cucumber, diced

3 tablespoons olive oil

1 tablespoon balsamic vinegar or lemon juice

extra herbs or flavour of your choice (see tip below)

Place the lettuce, spinach, tomatoes and cucumber in a salad bowl. Combine the olive oil and vinegar or lemon juice in a small jar with your chosen extra flavourings. Pop on the lid and give it a good shake. Pour over the salad and toss well.

Hints & Tips

✳ Options for flavouring your dressing are endless: you can add a pinch of chilli powder, ¼ teaspoon crushed garlic, a pinch of dried mint, ¼ teaspoon seeded mustard, salt and pepper or any combination! If you use lemon juice, you might want to add ¼ teaspoon sugar (balsamic is already sweetened).

Cheesy potato puff

This tasty recipe is another great way to use up leftover mashed potato and was sent in by Cassie Billingsley. Thanks, Cassie!

Serves 6 as a side

2 tablespoons breadcrumbs

3 eggs, beaten

6 cups mashed potato

¼ cup parsley leaves, finely chopped

salt and pepper

¾ cup grated cheese

Preheat the oven to 180°C and grease a small casserole or baking dish with butter. Sprinkle the breadcrumbs over the base of the dish to lightly coat.

In a large bowl, combine the mashed potato, eggs and parsley and mix well. Season to taste. Spread half of the potato mixture over the base of the casserole dish. Sprinkle over the cheese, then finish with the remaining potato mixture. Bake for 1 hour or until the top is golden. Serve hot.

Hints & Tips

* To make mash, wash, peel and chop 1.5 kg floury potatoes (5–6 large ones) and boil for 20 minutes in plenty of water. Drain and mash in the pot with ¼ cup of milk and 1 tablespoon of butter.

Mexican rice

Serves 4 as a side

2 tablespoons olive oil

1½ cups white long grain rice (e.g. basmati)

1 onion, diced

½ red capsicum, finely chopped

6 tablespoons tomato sauce

1 tablespoon taco seasoning

1 teaspoon crushed garlic

½ teaspoon chilli powder

Heat the olive oil in a heavy-based frying pan over medium heat. Add the rice and cook, stirring, for 3–4 minutes or until the rice is well coated and starts to brown. Remove from the heat and transfer to a bowl to cool.

Add the remaining ingredients to the pan along with 1½ cups water and return to the heat. Stir well and bring to the boil. Add the browned rice and stir. Cover and simmer on low for 30 minutes or until the rice is cooked through. Remove the lid, stir well and return to low heat for 10 minutes or until dried out. This dish is perfect with Homemade Baked Beans (page 138), or Honey-baked Chicken (page 257).

Cauliflower cheese

I love making cheese sauce in the microwave – it's not only faster, but you get a great consistency. I give my cauli stalks to my chooks, but you can use them to make Paleo Cauliflower Flatbread (page 159), which also works brilliantly as a pizza base.

Serves 4

1 head of cauliflower (about 1.5 kg), cut into florets

2 teaspoons butter

2 tablespoons plain flour

5 cups milk

1 teaspoon mustard powder (optional)

1½ cups grated cheese

salt and pepper

Place the cauliflower in a microwave-proof container with a little water. Microwave on high for 4–5 minutes or until tender. Drain and place in a casserole dish or baking dish with high sides.

Melt the butter in a jug in the microwave for 30–40 seconds until bubbling. Stir in the plain flour and microwave for an additional 20–30 seconds. Gently whisk in the milk and microwave for 1 minute. Whisk until the mixture starts to thicken. Add 1 cup of the grated cheese and the mustard powder (if using). Season to taste. Microwave for 30–60 seconds then whisk until the sauce is smooth and thick.

Pour the cheese sauce over the cauliflower and top with the remaining ½ cup of cheese. Place under a hot grill for 10 minutes until the top is golden and bubbling.

Cauliflower popcorn

Yet another delicious way to enjoy cauliflower, this one also makes a great snack.

Serves 4

1 head of cauliflower (about 1.5 kg), cut into bite-sized florets

⅓ cup olive oil

1 teaspoon sweet paprika

½ teaspoon turmeric

½ teaspoon cinnamon

salt and pepper

Preheat the oven to 200°C.

Pop the cauliflower florets into a large zip-lock bag. Add the oil and seasonings and carefully seal. Shake well to evenly coat the cauliflower.

Transfer to a baking tray and bake for 20 minutes. Remove from the oven, turn the florets and bake for another 10–15 minutes or until golden and crispy. Enjoy while hot!

Hints & Tips

✱ Don't throw away the stalk – roughly chop it and pop it in the freezer for making vegetable stock. You can also use it to make Paleo Cauliflower Flatbread (page 159).

Pasta

Pasta has got to be one of the quickest and
easiest go-to meals on the planet. You can cook
up big batches of it and keep leftovers in the fridge
for a couple days, plus there are all kinds of delicious
homemade sauces you can keep in the freezer ready
to go. For these recipes, I've gone with 350 g dried
pasta to serve four people, which is about 1½ cups
of cooked pasta each. If you have little ones,
you can drop that amount to 300 g, or even
250 g (exactly half a packet). The good thing
is that you can get high-fibre pasta, too,
which is good for the old gut.

Faster pasta

This meal is not only fast (it's ready in the time it takes to cook the pasta) but also incredibly frugal. Perfect for a weeknight meal.

Serves 4

350 g spaghetti

1 tablespoon olive oil

2 teaspoons crushed garlic

1 small onion, diced

250 g bacon rashers, diced

½ red capsicum, diced

1 teaspoon butter

chopped parsley, to serve

1 cup grated cheddar, to serve

Cook the spaghetti according to the packet instructions and keep warm.

Meanwhile, heat the olive oil in a frying pan over medium heat. Add the garlic and onion and cook for 5–8 minutes or until fragrant and soft. Add the bacon and capsicum and cook for 10 minutes or until the onion is starting to caramelise. Add the butter, allow to melt then add the cooked spaghetti. Stir well to combine. Serve with fresh parsley and grated cheese.

Hints & Tips

✳ To make this meal even cheaper I like to cook it the night before shopping day. It's a great meal to 'use up' anything left in the fridge. So don't strictly adhere to the recipe – use what you have! Other ingredients that work well include grated zucchini or carrot, or finely chopped mushrooms.

Tightwad macaroni special

Main meals really don't come much cheaper than this one!

Serves 4

350 g macaroni
(or any short pasta such as
penne, bowties, spirals)

1 × 425 g can tuna,
drained and flaked

1 × 420 g can cream of
chicken soup

1 cup frozen vegetables
(any kind)

grated cheese, to serve

Cook the pasta in a large saucepan or stockpot according to the packet directions.

Meanwhile, cook the frozen vegetables in the microwave according to the packet directions.

Drain the pasta and return it to the pan or pot over medium heat. Add the tuna and cream of chicken soup and stir gently to combine. When hot, mix in the cooked veggies. Serve immediately with grated cheese.

Leftover pasta bake

This is another great recipe to make the night before a food shop. Feel free to substitute any of the ingredients – it's all about using up the leftovers and bits and pieces in your fridge.

Serves 4

1 tablespoon butter

2 tablespoons plain flour

1 chicken stock cube, crushed

2 cups milk

1½ cups grated cheese

1 cup diced cooked meat (bacon, ham, turkey, chicken, etc.)

1 cup diced fresh tomatoes

1 cup sliced mushrooms

1 × 310 g can corn kernels

2 cups leftover cooked pasta (any kind)

Preheat the oven to 180°C.

Place the butter in a large microwave-proof jug and microwave on high for about 30–40 seconds or until melted and bubbling. Add the flour and stock cube and stir to make a roux (a fancy word for paste).

Whisk in ¼ cup of the milk and beat until smooth. Add the remaining milk and microwave on high for 1 minute at a time, whisking after each minute, until the mixture thickens. (This takes about 4 minutes, depending on your microwave.) Add 1 cup of the grated cheese and again whisk until smooth, microwaving for a further 30 seconds to melt the cheese if required.

In a casserole dish, place the meat, tomatoes, mushrooms, corn and cooked pasta and give it a good mix. Pour over the cheese sauce. Sprinkle over the remaining ½ cup of cheese and bake in the oven for 20 minutes or until bubbling and golden on top.

Pasta with basil crumble

I really love this simple way of cooking pasta. It's one of those recipes where you really need to use fresh herbs, so make sure you have fresh basil.

Serves 4

350 g pasta (any kind)

⅓ cup olive oil

2 teaspoons butter

3 teaspoons crushed garlic

1 cup breadcrumbs
(dry, not fresh)

1 small handful fresh basil leaves, finely chopped

grated parmesan, to serve
(optional)

Cook the pasta according to the packet directions. Drain and keep warm.

Heat the olive oil and butter in a large frying pan over medium–high heat. Add the garlic and cook for 30 seconds, stirring constantly. Reduce the heat to medium and pour in the breadcrumbs. Cook for a further 2–3 minutes, stirring well to absorb the oil.

Turn off the heat and add the basil and pasta, stirring gently to coat. Serve immediately topped with a sprinkle of parmesan if desired.

Tuna and pasta salad

This is a nice, easy lunch or dinner. The only thing that needs to be cooked is the pasta – and you could just as easily do that in the microwave (or use up some leftover pasta if you have some to hand).

Serves 1

100 g pasta (any kind)

1 × 90 g can tuna, flaked

¼ red onion, finely chopped

1 small carrot, grated

1 tablespoon mayo (see recipe page 80)

¼ cup grated cheese

Cook the pasta in a saucepan (or microwave) of salted boiling water until just tender. Drain and place in a serving bowl to cool.

Place the remaining ingredients in small bowl and mix well. Add to the pasta and stir until well combined. Serve immediately.

Schmancy macaroni cheese

When your family is on a super-tight budget, macaroni cheese is often a go-to recipe but it can get a bit boring – especially for the grown-ups. Rest assured this one is super fancy, delicious and easy to whip up in no time. Feel free to omit the ham if you need to reduce the cost.

Serves 4

350 g macaroni

2 large handfuls baby spinach

1 cup chopped cherry tomatoes

4 spring onions, finely sliced

1½ cups (250 g) diced ham (optional)

½ cup dried breadcrumbs

½ cup grated cheese

SAUCE

80 g butter

¼ cup plain flour

1½ cups milk

1 cup grated cheddar

1 tablespoon dijon mustard

1 tablespoon seeded wholegrain mustard

Preheat the oven to 180°C and grease a 24 cm round pie dish.

Follow the packet directions to cook the macaroni, drain and return to the pan to keep warm.

Meanwhile, to make the sauce, melt the butter in a saucepan over low heat. Add the flour and whisk to make a paste (roux). Cook for 2 minutes, whisking continuously. Slowly add the milk, turn up the heat to medium and continue whisking for 3 minutes or until the sauce starts to thicken. Stir through the cheddar and mustards and heat until the cheese melts.

Pour the sauce over the cooked macaroni. Stir through the spinach, tomato, spring onion and ham (if using) and pour into the prepared dish. Top with the breadcrumbs and cheese and bake for 25 minutes or until golden brown on top. Serve piping hot!

Slow-cooker ham and mushroom pasta

The ultimate in comfort food – perfect for a cold winter's night when you've got hungry mouths to feed.

Serves 4

1 × 420 g can cream of mushroom soup

1 × 375 ml can evaporated milk

2–3 cups (250 g) sliced mushrooms

2½ cups diced ham

salt and pepper

350 g fettuccini or tagliatelle (or other egg pasta)

1 spring onion, finely chopped

grated parmesan, to serve

Pour the soup and evaporated milk into the slow cooker. Add the mushrooms and ham and stir well. Season with salt and pepper. Cover and cook on low for 2 hours.

Close to serving time, cook the pasta according to the packet directions, drain well and add to the slow cooker. Mix well to coat. Stir through the spring onion and serve immediately with grated parmesan.

Pasta with tomato and zucchini

This is really a quick way to make your own passata. If you have some ripe tomatoes to hand, by all means use those instead of the tinned ones (they'll be sweeter).

Serves 4

350 g pasta (any kind)

1 teaspoon olive oil

1 teaspoon crushed garlic

1 small onion, diced

1 × 400 g can crushed tomatoes

2 zucchini, finely diced

1 teaspoon dried basil (optional)

grated parmesan or extra-tasty cheddar, to serve

Cook the pasta according to the packet directions. Drain and keep warm

In a small frying pan, heat the olive oil over medium heat. Add the garlic and onion and cook, stirring often, until soft and golden (5–8 minutes). Add the tomatoes, zucchini and basil (if using) and cook for 5–6 minutes or until the zucchini is soft and the liquid has reduced. Serve over the warm pasta with your choice of grated cheese.

Pasta with mushroom and garlic

I've made this sauce to serve two, but if your kids eat mushies, feel free to double the quantities.

Serves 2

175 g pasta (any kind)

1 tablespoon butter

½ teaspoon crushed garlic

1 cup sliced mushrooms

salt and pepper

2 tablespoons cream

Cook the pasta according to the packet directions. Drain and keep warm.

Meanwhile, heat the butter in a frying pan over medium–high heat. When sizzling, add the garlic and cook for 30 seconds or so. Add the mushrooms and cook, stirring often, for 5 minutes or until the mushies are soft and browned. Season with salt and pepper and take off the heat. Add the cream and mix well. Spoon over the warm pasta and enjoy.

Pasta with bacon, tomato and white wine

This sauce is really delicious, though if you're feeding kids, substitute the white wine with ½ cup water mixed with 1 teaspoon of sugar.

Serves 4

350 g pasta (any kind)

¼ cup olive oil

1 onion, finely diced

3 bacon rashers, finely diced

1 × 400 g can chopped tomatoes

½ cup white wine

1 teaspoon chilli flakes (optional)

Cook the pasta according to the packet directions. Drain and keep warm.

Meanwhile, heat the olive oil in a frying pan over medium heat. When hot, add the onion and cook until softened but not brown (about 5–6 minutes). Add the bacon and fry for 3–4 minutes, stirring often, until cooked through. Stir in the tomatoes, wine and chilli (if using). Reduce heat and simmer for 10 minutes until the liquid reduces to make a nice thick sauce. Serve over warm pasta – yum!

Frugal carbonara

This one is always a crowd pleaser!

Serves 4

350 g pasta (any kind)

1 teaspoon butter

1 teaspoon crushed garlic

1 small onion, diced

4 bacon rashers, finely chopped

½ cup thickened cream

salt and pepper

½ cup grated cheddar

Cook the pasta according to the packet directions. Drain and keep warm.

Heat the butter in a frying pan over medium heat. When sizzling, add the garlic, onion and bacon and cook for about 10 minutes, stirring often, until the bacon is crisp. Turn the heat down to the lowest setting. Stir in the cream and season to taste. Add the cheese and stir until just beginning to melt. Remove from the heat, add the pasta and stir to coat. Serve immediately.

Pasta in lemon and basil sauce

Basil and pasta are a match made in heaven. If you have fresh basil growing in your yard, take advantage of it and regularly make fresh pesto sauce (page 88) – it is simply delicious over pasta. This version is a fresh, lemony basil sauce perfect for the summer months. It is served with cold pasta.

Serves 4

350 g pasta (any kind)

1 cup basil leaves, coarsely chopped

2 tablespoons olive oil

juice of 2 lemons, plus zest of ½ lemon

1 teaspoon crushed garlic

½ cup finely grated parmesan

Cook the pasta according to the packet directions. Drain, place in a serving bowl and set aside to cool completely.

Place the remaining ingredients in a bowl or jug and mix well. Pour over the pasta and toss to combine. Refrigerate for 30 minutes to chill and serve cold.

Pasta with spicy pumpkin sauce

Pumpkin puree is a delicious and versatile ingredient to keep in the freezer, so I reckon it's worth chopping up a whole pumpkin and baking it for this recipe – you may as well while you've got the oven on! Freeze the leftover puree for pumpkin soup, pumpkin scones or to add to any casserole or sauce for a hit of smooth sweetness.

Serves 4

350 g pasta (any kind)

500 g pumpkin, deseeded and cut into wedges (makes about 1 cup puree)

2 tablespoons cream

½ cup coconut cream (optional)

1 teaspoon curry powder

Preheat the oven to 190°C.

Arrange the pumpkin wedges on a baking tray and bake for 20 minutes or until the skins are well browned and the flesh is soft.

Meanwhile, cook the pasta according to the packet directions. Drain and keep warm.

Remove the pumpkin from the oven and allow to cool slightly before peeling off the skins. Place the flesh in a blender with the cream, coconut cream (if using) and curry powder then puree. Transfer to a microwave-proof jug and heat on high for 1 minute or until nearly boiling. Pour over the pasta and enjoy.

Hints & Tips

* To make bulk **Pumpkin Puree**, bake extra pumpkin wedges as per the method. Set them aside to cool, puree in batches and freeze flat in 1-cup portions in zip-lock bags. They will last for 3 months.

* To make **Pasta with Spicy Cauliflower Sauce**, simply steam 500 g cauliflower instead of baking the pumpkin and follow the rest of the method. Too easy!

Snag dishes

Sausages are a big part of our culture and
an easy way to feed hordes of hungry kids at sporting
events and barbecues. I know many of us like to think
we've outgrown snags, but at around $6 a kilo, they're
the ultimate in frugal cooking for meat lovers. These
recipes are simple, cheap and easy!

Fried sausage and potato cook up

This may be a super-cheap recipe, but it is actually really tasty. Add a few veggies from the garden and you have a decent meal!

Serves 4

4 large potatoes, peeled and cut into cubes

2 tablespoons butter

2–3 sausages (pork or beef)

1 onion, cut into eighths

Place the potatoes in a microwave-proof container with a little water. Microwave on high for 10 minutes or until just tender. Drain well.

Meanwhile, heat the butter in a frying pan over medium heat. Add the sausages and onion and fry for 10–12 minutes or until the sausages are just cooked. Remove pan from the heat.

Transfer the sausages to a chopping board and leave to cool slightly before slicing into small pieces. Return to the pan with the potato. Turn up the heat to medium–hot and cook for 2–3 minutes to brown the potatoes and sausages. Serve with a fresh salad.

Sticky sausages

Be bored with sausages *no more*! Sticky sausages are easy to make and only contain a couple of very simple ingredients.

Serves 4–6

10 sausages (any kind you like)

1 tablespoon oil

4 tablespoons brown sugar

2 teaspoons crushed garlic

200 ml tomato sauce

salt and pepper

Preheat the oven to 180°C and line a baking tray with baking paper.

Arrange the sausages on the tray and bake for 20 minutes or until browned. Pour off any excess oil. Cut each sausage in half to make 20 little sausages.

Combine the remaining ingredients in a jug and mix well. Pour over the sausages and bake for a further 10 minutes or until the sausages become caramelised and sticky. Serve with mashed potato and steamed vegetables.

Hints & Tips

✳ To make this meal even cheaper, use fewer sausages and serve with more vegetables and rice instead of potatoes.

The world's best curried sausages

This recipe is courtesy of Clancy Briggs, who always said that her mother made the best curried sausages in the whole world – and the easiest. One call to her mum got us this super simple and frugal recipe that's sure to become your new family favourite. These are delicious served with mashed potato, but you can also serve them with brown rice or Smashed Garlic Potatoes (page 210).

Serves 4–6

8 sausages (any sort!)

1 onion, diced

¾ cup sugar

1 teaspoon brown sugar

1 teaspoon curry powder, or to taste

1 tablespoon cornflour

Heat a deep frying pan over medium–high heat and fry the sausages for 5 minutes, turning often, until nicely browned (this adds that extra caramelised taste). Reduce the heat to medium, add the onion, sugars, curry powder and 2 cups of water and bring to a simmer. Cook for 10–15 minutes, or until the sausages are cooked through.

In a small cup mix the cornflour with 1 teaspoon of water to make a paste. Add the paste to the pan, stirring well, and cook for 4–5 minutes or until the sauce thickens. Serve over mashed potato with steamed vegetables.

Sausage stroganoff

Always looking for new and different ways to serve snags? Look no further. Sausage stroganoff works equally well with beef or pork sausages.

Serves 4–6

1 tablespoon olive oil

8 beef or pork sausages

1 onion, finely chopped

2 teaspoons crushed garlic

1 cup sliced mushrooms (any kind)

2 tablespoons tomato paste

1 tablespoon paprika

1 cup beef stock (or 1 beef stock cube dissolved in 1 cup boiling water)

½ cup sour cream

salt and pepper

Heat the oil in a heavy-based frying pan over medium heat. Fry the sausages for 10 minutes, turning often, or until cooked through and well browned. Remove from the pan, chop into smaller pieces and set aside.

Add the onion, garlic and mushrooms to the pan and cook for 10 minutes, stirring often, until browned and soft. Stir in the tomato paste, paprika and stock and bring to a simmer. Return the sausages to the pan and simmer for 5–6 minutes or until heated through. Turn off the heat and stir in the sour cream. Season to taste. Serve over pasta or rice with a side of steamed vegetables.

Hints & Tips

* To make it even cheaper, use tomato sauce instead of the tomato paste and evaporated milk instead of sour cream.

Sausage risotto

This dish is soooo easy to make, super frugal and is suitable for freezing, too! Great for any time of year, but works a treat in the colder months. Italian sausages are pork sausages flavoured with fennel and garlic and should be pretty easy to find in any supermarket.

Serves 4–6

¼ cup olive oil

1 onion, diced

1 teaspoon crushed garlic

1½ cups arborio rice

2½ cups chicken stock

1 × 400 g can crushed tomatoes

8 Italian sausages

50 g parmesan, finely grated

¼ cup chopped parsley

Preheat the oven to 180°C.

Heat the oil (reserving 1 teaspoon) in a heavy-based, ovenproof saucepan (or flame-proof casserole dish) over medium heat. Sauté the onion and garlic for 5–8 minutes, stirring often, until fragrant and tender. Add the rice and cook for 2–3 minutes or until well coated. Add the stock and tomatoes, cover with the lid and transfer to the oven for 30 minutes or until the rice is cooked through.

Meanwhile, heat the remaining teaspoon of oil in a frying pan over medium heat and pan-fry the sausages for 10 minutes, turning regularly, until they are nice and brown and cooked through. Transfer to a chopping board and cut into bite-sized pieces.

When the rice is cooked, remove from the oven, add the sausage pieces and stir in the cheese and parsley. Serve immediately.

Hints & Tips

* To freeze leftovers (ensure they are cool first), place in a zip-lock bag, label and date and freeze for up to 6 months.

Hot dog casserole

If you have a barbecue one night and have some leftover snags, don't give them to the dog! Cover them in plastic wrap and make this for dinner the next night – it's a great favourite with the kids.

Serves 4–6 kids

6 hotdog buns

¼ cup tomato sauce

1 tablespoon mild mustard

6 cooked sausages

1 cup grated cheddar

Preheat the oven to 170°C and line a large baking tray with foil.

Make a cut lengthways along the centre of each bun, stopping just before you reach the bottom.

Combine the tomato sauce and mustard in a cup and mix well. Spread each cut side of the buns with the sauce mixture. Place a sausage in each bun and top with cheese. Bake for 10–15 minutes or until the cheese is golden brown and the buns are toasted. Serve immediately.

Hints & Tips

✳ You can use any style of mustard if you like: American-style, wholegrain, dijon or even a hot English mustard if your kids don't mind the flavour.

✳ This recipe is not suitable for freezing.

Slow-cooker Italian sausage and bean stew

In this recipe, I'm using the slightly spicier Italian pork sausages that are made with fennel, garlic and chilli. Look for them in the deli section of supermarkets, or at your local butcher.

Serves 4–6

1 tablespoon olive oil

5 thick Italian-style sausages

2 tablespoons crushed garlic

1 large capsicum, finely diced

2 × 400 g cans crushed tomatoes

1 × 400 g can borlotti beans, drained and rinsed well

1 teaspoon paprika

Heat the oil in a frying pan over medium heat and fry the sausages for 10 minutes, turning often, or until browned on all sides, then transfer to a chopping board.

Cut into bite-sized pieces and transfer to the slow cooker with the remaining ingredients. Cook on low for 5 hours, stirring every hour or so. If the mixture thickens too quickly, add ¼ cup of water. Serve with mashed potatoes and steamed vegetables.

Slow-cooker coconut curry sausages

This is a family favourite that we would have once a week in the colder weather. It is so delicious and hearty, yet will easily feed a family for under $10. It even freezes well, too! Recipe by Jodie Tydings in Gympie.

Serves 4–6

500 g pork sausages, sliced

1 small onion, diced

1 teaspoon crushed garlic

500 g mixed vegetables, chopped (e.g. pumpkin, zucchini, choko, potato, carrot)

1 × 400 ml can coconut cream

2 tablespoons curry powder

Put the sausages, onion, garlic and vegetables in the slow cooker. In a small jug mix together the coconut cream and curry powder and pour over the top. Cook on low for 6 hours or until the sausages are tender. Serve with rice or over pasta.

Mince dishes

Mince (particularly minced beef) is the hero
in this chapter and, at around $8 a kilo, it comes in
second after the humble snag as the frugal choice
for meat lovers. Of course, like with any ingredient,
buying in bulk is a great option if you have a large
enough freezer. And remember that 'mince' doesn't
only refer to beef: supermarkets now stock chicken
mince, pork mince or even a combination of
pork and beef, which makes a fantastic
spaghetti bolognaise sauce.

Bulk slow-cooked mince

If you're cooking for four people, it doesn't make much sense to put a 3 kg slab of mince in the freezer! Dividing it into portions is one option, but an even better way to save time and money is to cook up the lot in advance. If you have a 6 litre slow cooker, you should be able to cook up a 3 kg pack in three lots.

Makes 10 portions

3 kg mince

Place mince in your slow cooker until three-quarters full. Set the cooker to auto (or low if you don't have an auto setting), add a cup of water and place the lid on. Cook for 6 hours or until the mince is thoroughly browned. Give it a good stir every hour or so.

Turn off the slow cooker and leave it to sit until the mince is cool enough to handle. Place 300 g portions into zip-lock bags, flattening them and gently pressing out as much air as possible before sealing (flat portions stack easily). Cooked mince will last in the freezer for up to 6 months.

Golden bake

This is basically a frugal shepherd's pie – very simple and very delicious.

Serves 4

4 potatoes (about 750 g), peeled and quartered

250 g peeled and deseeded pumpkin, cut into chunks

pinch of salt

2 tablespoons butter

2 onions, diced

500 g mince (beef or pork – whatever is on sale)

2 tablespoons plain flour

1 tablespoon gravy mix (see page 85)

1 cup grated cheese

Preheat the oven to 180°C and grease a 24cm pie dish.

Place the potato and pumpkin in a large saucepan. Cover with water and add a pinch of salt. Bring to the boil over medium heat and cook for 12 minutes or until the potato is tender. Drain. Add 1 tablespoon of the butter to the pan and mash until smooth.

Heat the remaining tablespoon of butter in a frying pan over medium heat. Add the onion and mince and cook for 8–10 minutes, breaking up the mince with a wooden spoon. Add the flour and gravy mix and cook, stirring, for 1–2 minutes to get the 'floury taste' out. Add 1½ cups of water and continue heating and stirring until the sauce is nice and thick (about 5–6 minutes). Transfer the mince mixture to the pie dish and top with the mashed potato and pumpkin. Sprinkle the cheese evenly over the top and bake for 25–30 minutes or until the cheese is melted and bubbling and starting to brown.

Hints & Tips

✳ This works just as well with potatoes only, or with sweet potatoes or even a mixture of potato and parsnip – use whatever is cheapest or is in your vegetable crisper.

Traditional Aussie rissoles

I loved rissoles as a kid and I love them now. They are easy to make, very tasty, and always a hit with the kids. So what's the difference between rissoles and hamburger patties? Not a lot in my book, though rissoles are a bit smaller and chunkier.

Makes about 8

½ cup flour

500 g minced beef

½ onion, finely chopped

1 × 40 g packet French onion soup mix

¾ cup breadcrumbs (dry or fresh)

1 egg

Place the flour in a shallow bowl and set aside until needed.

Combine the remaining ingredients in a bowl and mix well. Scoop out heaped tablespoonsful of the mixture and form into 5 cm wide rissoles. Carefully roll in the flour and transfer to a plate. Cover with plastic wrap and refrigerate for 30 minutes to firm up.

Heat a non-stick frying pan over medium heat and cook the rissoles for 5 minutes on each side or until browned and cooked through. Serve with Rosemary Potatoes (page 211) and steamed vegetables or on Homemade Bread Rolls (page 91) with salad.

Hints & Tips

 * This mixture makes delicious meatballs – simply roll heaped teaspoonsful into balls and cook for 5 minutes, moving them around in the pan so they cook on all sides.

 * To freeze, allow the meatballs to cool to room temperature. Place in zip-lock bags, label, date and freeze for up to 6 months.

Cheesy beef and macaroni bake

Another crowd pleaser, this costs under $10 to make so is easy on the hip pocket.

Serves 4–6

canola oil spray

1 teaspoon oil or butter

1 onion, finely diced

1 teaspoon crushed garlic

500 g minced beef

1 tablespoon Worcestershire sauce

2 teaspoons dried mixed herbs

2 × 400 g cans crushed tomatoes

350 g (2 cups) macaroni

pinch of salt

1½ cups grated cheddar

TO GARNISH (OPTIONAL)

125 g cherry tomatoes (½ a punnet)

12 basil leaves

3 rosemary sprigs

Preheat the oven to 180°C. Lightly spray a large baking dish or casserole dish with canola oil spray.

Heat the oil or butter in a frying pan over medium heat and fry the onion and garlic for 5 minutes or until soft. Add the mince and cook, stirring to break up clumps, for about 10 minutes or until browned. Add the Worcestershire sauce, herbs and tomatoes. Reduce the heat to low and simmer, uncovered, for 10 minutes or until the sauce thickens.

Meanwhile, cook the macaroni in a large pot of salted boiling water for 12–15 minutes or until just tender. Drain well.

Spread half of the mince mixture over the base of the prepared dish. Top with the pasta, followed by the remaining mince mixture. Sprinkle with grated cheese and bake for 15 minutes or until the cheese is starting to brown.

Hints & Tips

* For fancy cheesy beef and macaroni pies, layer the ingredients in four large ramekins (or six smaller ones), cut puff pastry to fit the tops, and bake in a 190°C oven for 20 minutes or until the puff pastry is golden.

Spaghetti pie

Sick of boring old spag bol? Try this twist on an old favourite. Super tasty and frugal, and who doesn't need another mince recipe in their repertoire? This is another good way to use up leftover cooked pasta.

Serves 4–6

350 g spaghetti

4 egg whites

⅓ cup grated parmesan

1 tablespoon olive oil

2¾ cups (340 g) cottage cheese, placed in a fine sieve to drain

250 g minced beef

1 cup sliced mushrooms

1 onion, chopped

2 teaspoons crushed garlic

1 × 400 g can crushed tomatoes

1½ teaspoons mixed herbs

½ teaspoon salt, plus salt and pepper to taste

½ cup grated cheddar

canola oil spray

Cooked the spaghetti according to the packet instructions and set aside.

Preheat the oven to 180°C and grease a 24 cm pie dish.

In a bowl, whisk together two of the egg whites. Add the parmesan, olive oil and cooked spaghetti, toss to coat. Press the spaghetti mixture evenly into the base and sides of the prepared dish.

In another bowl, combine the remaining egg whites and cottage cheese. Spread the mixture over the pasta 'crust'.

Grease a large frying pan with a little canola oil spray and cook the mince, mushrooms, onion and garlic until the meat is brown (about 10 minutes). Stir in the tomatoes, mixed herbs and salt and mix well. Spoon over the cottage cheese mixture and bake for 20 minutes. Remove from the oven, sprinkle with cheddar and season to taste. Bake for a further 5 minutes or until the cheese is melted. Allow to stand for 5–10 minutes before serving.

Porcupine meatballs

Kids love these – they are not only inexpensive, but filling and very tasty!

Serves 4

500 g minced beef

½ cup long grain rice
(e.g. basmati)

1 onion, finely diced

1 teaspoon crushed garlic

1 egg

1 × 420 g can tomato
soup

Preheat the oven to 180°C.

Place the mince, rice, onion, garlic and egg in a bowl and mix well. Roll dessertspoonfuls into balls and place in a large casserole dish or pie dish.

Place the tomato soup and 1 cup of water in a microwave-proof bowl and microwave on high for 2–3 minutes or until hot. Stir well and pour over the meatballs. Bake, uncovered, for 30 minutes or until the rice in the meatballs is cooked. Serve with a side of mash or roast veggies.

Hints & Tips

✳ Check after 15 minutes to see if there is still plenty of liquid in the dish (sometimes the rice absorbs it too quickly). If it's drying out, add an extra ½ cup of water to the pan.

Traditional spaghetti bolognaise

Fresh basil and tomatoes make all the difference to this family staple.

Serves 4

1 tablespoon olive oil

2 cloves garlic, crushed

250 g (about 2) tomatoes, roughly chopped

1 × 400 g can diced tomatoes

2 tablespoons chopped basil leaves

salt, to taste

2 teaspoons dried oregano

500 g minced beef

350 g spaghetti

grated parmesan, to serve (optional)

Heat the oil in a large saucepan over medium–high heat. Add the garlic and sauté for 30 seconds or until golden. Add the tomatoes, basil and salt. Reduce heat to low, cover and cook for 10 minutes. Using a stick blender, blend the tomato mixture until smooth then add the oregano.

Place a frying pan over medium–high heat and cook the mince for 5–6 minutes. Use a wooden spoon or fork to break up the mince and move it around the pan so that it browns on all sides and doesn't clump together. Tip the mince into the pan with the tomatoes and stir to combine. Cover and cook over low heat for 1½ hours, stirring occasionally.

To prepare the pasta, fill a large saucepan with water, bring to the boil and season with salt. Add the spaghetti and cook for 8–10 minutes or until al dente. Drain. Serve the sauce over the pasta with a sprinkle of grated parmesan, if desired.

Hints & Tips

* If you don't have fresh basil, use 2 teaspoons of dried basil.

Shepherd's pie

The soft potato topping and succulent meaty middle makes this
a family favourite.

Serves 6

TOPPING

3 large potatoes, peeled
and quartered

¼ cup hot milk

1 tablespoon butter

1 chicken stock cube,
crumbled

¾ cup grated cheddar

FILLING

1 teaspoon olive oil

750 g minced beef or
lamb

1 onion, diced

1 teaspoon crushed garlic

1 carrot, diced

1 tablespoon tomato paste

1 teaspoon Worcestershire
sauce

1 beef stock cube,
crumbled

1 teaspoon soy sauce
(optional)

1 tablespoon plain flour

To make the topping, place the potatoes in a large
saucepan and cover with water. Bring to the boil
and cook for 20 minutes or until the potatoes are
very tender. Drain. Add the hot milk, butter and
stock cube. Mash until light and fluffy.

To make the mince filling, heat the oil in a heavy-
based frying pan over medium–high heat. Add the
mince, onion, garlic and carrot, then cook, stirring
frequently, until the mince is well browned and
the vegetables are soft (about 15 minutes). Add the
tomato paste, Worcestershire sauce, stock cube
and soy sauce (if using) along with ¾ cup water.
Stir well and bring the mixture to the boil. Reduce
heat and simmer, uncovered for 3–4 minutes.
Stir in the flour and cook for 5 minutes to thicken,
adding a little extra water if the mixture is too
thick.

Spoon the mince mixture into a large casserole
or pie dish. Spread the mashed potato over the
top and sprinkle over the cheese. Place under the
grill for 10 minutes or until the cheese is golden
brown. Serve immediately.

Hints & Tips

✱ To freeze, place slices in a freezer-proof
container for up to 4 months.

Slow-cooker lasagne

Making lasagne in the slow cooker is perfect for entertaining or just making large batches to freeze for another night.

Serves 6–8

1 × 250 g packet lasagne sheets

BÉCHAMEL SAUCE (FANCY CHEESE SAUCE)

1 tablespoon butter

1 tablespoon plain flour

2 cups milk

1 chicken stock cube, crumbled

salt and pepper

1 cup grated cheddar (mild or tasty), plus extra for the top

MINCE FILLING

500 g minced beef

1 onion, diced

1 × 400 g can diced tomatoes

1 tablespoon crushed garlic

2 tablespoons tomato paste

1 tablespoon sugar

salt and pepper

1 teaspoon dried oregano

1 teaspoon dried basil

Hints & Tips

✳ To make this meal even cheaper use generic branded lasagne sheets, milk and cheese.

✳ You can leave out the chicken stock cube in the cheese sauce if you wish, but it does make it taste truly spectacular!

Grease the inside of your slow cooker (I use canola spray) to prevent the lasagne from sticking to the sides. Preheat the cooker on low.

To make the cheese sauce, place the butter and flour in a microwave-proof jug and cook on high for 1 minute or until the mixture starts to become foamy and the butter is melted. Remove from the microwave and whisk until well combined. Add the milk, ¼ cup at a time, and microwave for 30 second stints, whisking in between each addition. When you've almost added all of the milk, add the stock cube and season to taste with salt and pepper. Add the cheese and cook for another 60–90 seconds then whisk until the sauce is lovely, smooth and thickened.

To make the mince filling, place all of the ingredients in a large bowl and mix well.

To assemble, spoon one-third of the mince mixture into the base of the slow cooker. Place a layer of lasagne sheets over the top without overlapping (you may have to break off corners to make them fit). Next, pour half of the cheese sauce over the pasta sheets and top with another third of the mince mixture. Place a second layer of lasagne sheets over the mince and pour over the remaining cheese sauce. Finish with the remaining meat mixture. Sprinkle a little extra cheese on top. Cook on low for 6 hours or on high for 4 hours.

To serve, use a large serving spoon to 'scoop' out the lasagne. Serve with Leafy Green Salad (page 212) and Garlic Bread (page 59).

Mario's meatballs with milk

You haven't eaten good meatballs until you've tried this version. You may think it odd that our meatballs are made with milk, but milk breaks down the enzymes in the meat to make it lovely and tender.

Serves 4

500 g minced beef

1 onion, finely diced

1 cup breadcrumbs

½ cup milk

1 egg, beaten

2 tablespoons tomato sauce

STICKY MEATBALL SAUCE

2 tablespoons mustard pickles

1 × 400 g can tomato soup

1 onion, diced

2 tablespoons brown sugar

1 tablespoon white vinegar

1 tablespoon Worcestershire sauce

Preheat the oven to 180°C.

Place the mince, onion, breadcrumbs, milk, egg and tomato sauce in a bowl and mix really well. Take heaped teaspoonsful of the mixture and shape into balls. Pop on a plate while you make the sauce.

In a saucepan, combine all of the sauce ingredients with ½ cup water and heat over medium–low heat until the onion is softened and the sugar melted. Use a stick blender to process in the pan until nice and smooth (or transfer to a food processor).

Place the meatballs in a casserole or baking dish and pour the sticky sauce over the top. Bake for 1 hour or until the meatballs are brown and the sauce thickens and caramelises. Stir once or twice during baking. Enjoy the best meatballs you've ever tasted! They are delicious with rice, pasta or any potato-based side dish.

Chook dishes

Australians love chook – we actually
have the world's third-highest consumption
of chicken (after Malaysia and Jamaica). This may
have something to do with the fact that chicken meat,
on average, is 50 per cent cheaper than pork,
59 per cent cheaper than lamb and 65 per cent
cheaper than beef. It is also very versatile and
quite easy to cook compared to other meats.

Sweet soy drumsticks

These can be a bit messy to prepare, but they are really yummy – and the kids love them. Chicken drumsticks can be picked up for as little as $3 a kilo. And these are so quick to make that you'll have time to make a delicious side dish, such as Sweet Potato Mash (page 142), or Fried Rice (page 182). Recipe by Chadaporn Pickford.

Serves 4

8 chicken drumsticks

½ cup sweet soy sauce

1 cup cornflour

Preheat the oven to 180°C and line a baking tray with baking paper.

Pour the soy sauce into one shallow bowl, and the cornflour in another. Coat each chicken leg first in the sauce, then in the cornflour (yes it might start falling off, but do the best you can). Quickly transfer to the prepared tray. Bake for 35 minutes or until golden and cooked through. Serve with plain rice and cooked frozen vegetables.

Chicken rice casserole

This casserole is perfect for when you have some leftover chicken in the fridge – it's a great family meal for a weeknight dinner.

Serves 4

1½ cups white rice

2 cups chicken stock

2 cups broccoli florets

2 cups leftover cooked chicken, shredded

1 cup sour cream

1 × 420 g can cream of chicken soup

2 cups cornflakes, crushed

¼ cup butter, melted

canola oil spray

Preheat the oven to 180°C. Lightly grease a large casserole dish with canola oil spray.

Spread the rice evenly over the base of the casserole dish. Pour over the stock then add the broccoli and chicken.

In a jug, whisk the sour cream and soup until well combined, and pour evenly over the top of the chicken.

Place the crushed cornflakes in a bowl and pour over the melted butter. Stir to coat. Spoon the cornflake mixture over the chicken and broccoli. Bake for 30–40 minutes or until the top is crunchy and golden brown.

Strapped-for-cash chicken supreme

We ate this meal many times during our four years living on $50 a week. With a few different herbs and spices, it can taste a little different every time. And the kids really liked it, too!

Serves 4

1 kg chicken pieces (drumsticks and wings are the cheapest)

1 × 420 g can cream of chicken soup

1 cup frozen mixed vegetables

1 teaspoon dried herb of your choice (e.g. tarragon, parsley)

salt and pepper

Preheat the oven to 180°C.

Place the chicken pieces in a baking dish or casserole dish and bake for 25 minutes or until just about cooked through. Remove from the oven and either strip the meat off the bone and return it to the dish, or if the kids don't mind eating chicken off the bone, just leave the browned pieces whole.

Add the soup, frozen vegetables and herbs, and season to taste with a little salt and pepper. Return to the oven and bake for 15–20 minutes or until bubbly. Serve with steamed rice.

Hints & Tips

✳ Use 500 g of chicken thighs or breasts if you prefer. Just reduce the browning time to 20 minutes.

✳ For a bit of crunch, mix 1 cup of fresh breadcrumbs (see page 62) with a tablespoon of melted butter and sprinkle over the top before baking.

Honey-baked chicken

Only four simple ingredients in this recipe – yet it's so scrumptious!

Serves 4

1 kg chicken pieces

¾ cup white wine or chicken stock

¼ cup honey

1 × 40 g packet French onion soup mix

Preheat the oven to 160°C.

Place the chicken pieces in a large baking dish or round casserole dish.

Place the white wine or chicken stock, honey and soup mix in a jug and stir until well combined. Pour over the chicken pieces. Cover with foil (or pop on the lid) and bake for 1 hour. Remove the foil or lid, increase the heat to 200°C and brown for 10 minutes. Serve with plain steamed rice or Fried Rice (page 182) and steamed Asian vegetables.

Hints & Tips

✳ This will last in an airtight container in the fridge for 2 days, or in the freezer for up to 3 months.

Super healthy chicken meatloaf

This is no traditional stodgy meatloaf! It's super healthy, especially served with salad and a dollop of Greek yogurt. It's also really yummy sliced on sandwiches for lunch the next day. I use silverbeet, as it is so easy to grow in the garden, but feel free to use spinach if you have some.

Serves 4

500 g chicken mince

1 cup breadcrumbs

½ cup pine nuts
(optional – pine nuts are expensive!)

½ cup (100 g) crumbled feta

2 eggs, lightly beaten

3 silverbeet leaves, finely chopped

2 teaspoons lemon zest

2 teaspoons crushed garlic

2 tablespoons mayo

Preheat the oven to 180°C. Line a large loaf tin with baking paper.

Place all of the ingredients in a large bowl and mix thoroughly (I use my hands!). Transfer the mixture to the loaf tin, forming it into a log shape in the centre of the tin. Smooth over the top with clean, damp hands. Bake for 45 minutes or until the outside is just starting to brown. Leave to rest for 15 minutes before slicing.

Hints & Tips

* Nuts give this a wholesome chewy texture, so instead of pine nuts, you could use chopped cashews or walnuts.

* To freeze, allow the meatloaf to cool to room temperature. Cover in plastic wrap and freeze for up to 3 months.

Caramelised chicken and tomato casserole

Another delicious, super-cheap, fast family favourite.

Serves 4

1 kg chicken pieces

¼ cup soy sauce

2 teaspoons crushed garlic

2 teaspoons brown sugar

1 × 420 g can tomato soup

Preheat the oven to 180°C.

Arrange the chicken pieces in the base of a casserole dish. In a jug, mix together the remaining ingredients and pour over the top. Cover with a lid or foil and bake for 1 hour.

Serve with mashed potato and steamed vegetables.

Chicken and cauliflower bake

When I hear the words 'creamy sauce' a little part of me dances! Here's my twist on an old favourite – and you won't even have to stand at the stove and stir it for 10 minutes.

Serves 4

500 g chicken breast fillets

1 head of cauliflower (about 1.5 kg), cored and quartered

2 rashers bacon, diced

3 spring onions, finely chopped

2 teaspoons crushed garlic

2 cups grated cheddar

½ cup crumbled blue cheese (optional, but delectable)

Preheat the oven to 180°C.

Place the chicken breast in a large saucepan or stockpot and cover with boiling water. Place over medium–low heat and simmer, covered, for 5 minutes. Add the cauliflower and enough boiling water to cover. Cook, covered, for 15 minutes or until the cauliflower is tender and the chicken is cooked through. Drain, cool slightly and dice.

Place the cooked, diced chicken and cauliflower in a casserole dish. Add the spring onion, bacon and garlic and stir well to combine. Add 1½ cups of the grated cheese and the blue cheese (if using) and mix well. Sprinkle the remaining ½ cup of cheese over the top. Cover with foil and bake for 20 minutes. Remove the foil and bake for another 5 minutes to brown the top. Serve with steamed broccoli, beans, peas and carrots.

Hints & Tips

✳ To make this meal even cheaper, use chicken thigh pieces instead of breast fillets and omit the blue cheese

Slow-cooker roast chicken

Having some leftover roast chicken makes life very easy – use it in soups, salads, sandwiches and wraps. (See my recipe for homemade tortillas on page 92.) If you have cooked chicken in the fridge, you always have a meal!

Serves 4

1 whole chicken (any size)

1 tablespoon crushed garlic

2 tablespoons butter

Grab a small saucer and place it upside down in the base of the slow cooker – this will hold your chicken up out of the juices so it doesn't break apart too much. Place the chicken on top of the saucer. Mix the garlic and butter together and slather over the chicken. Cook on low for 4–6 hours. The meat will just fall off the bone. Serve with Rosemary Potatoes (page 211), Rice Pilaf (page 202) or your favourite veggie sides.

Hints & Tips

* If you want to use a frozen whole chicken, you must allow it to thaw completely in the fridge first.

* To make the skin brown and crispy, preheat the oven to 190°C. Carefully transfer the chicken from the slow cooker to a baking tray and bake for 10 minutes.

Slow-cooker lemon chicken

Once you've made one slow-cooker chicken recipe, it's hard to go back to cooking chook any other way. This is another firm favourite!

Serves 4–6

8 chicken pieces

2 teaspoons crushed garlic

2 teaspoons dried oregano

salt and pepper

½ cup white wine or chicken stock

juice and zest of 1 lemon

Place the chicken pieces in a bowl with the garlic and 1 teaspoon of the oregano. Toss to coat and season to taste with salt and pepper.

Heat a large non-stick frying pan over medium–high heat and fry the chicken pieces for 8 minutes, or until browned. Transfer to the slow cooker together with any pan juices. Pour over the wine or chicken stock and add the remaining teaspoon of oregano. Cover and cook on low for 6 hours.

In the final hour of cooking, add the lemon juice and zest. Serve with mashed potato or pasta and steamed vegetables.

Slow-cooker creamy salsa chicken

Deliciously spicy. Pop it on in the morning and it's ready when you get home from work.

Serves 4

1 kg chicken pieces

2 cups tomato salsa (see page 180)

1 × 30 g packet taco seasoning mix

½ cup sour cream, to serve

Place the chicken, salsa, taco seasoning and ¼ cup water in the slow cooker and cook on high for 4 hours (or on low for 6 hours). Serve topped with the sour cream and a side of steamed rice.

Slow-cooker apricot chicken

This was one of the very first meals I made in a slow cooker, and it is still a favourite with the kiddies. I serve it on brown rice, as the nutty flavour goes really well with the sweet apricots.

Serves 4–6

1 onion, cut into rings

1 kg chicken pieces or 8 chicken drumsticks

1 × 40 g packet French onion soup mix

1 × 840 g can apricots

Place the onion rings in the base of the slow cooker and arrange the chicken pieces on top. Sprinkle over the French onion soup mix. Pour over the apricots and the syrup. Cook on low for 4–5 hours or until the chicken is tender and starts to fall off the bone. Serve with brown rice.

Hints & Tips

✳ To make a delicious **Apricot Chicken Curry**, add 1–2 teaspoons curry powder (depending on your taste).

Slow-cooker broccoli cheesy chicken

A sweet and creamy recipe that will coax even the most reluctant broccoli eater. The stems are actually sweet and tender, too, so dice them up and pop them in as well.

Serves 4

2 chicken breasts, cut into 1.5 cm cubes

2 tablespoons butter

125 g (½ cup) cream cheese

1 × 420 g can cream of celery soup

¼ cup milk

½ head of broccoli (about 500 g), cut into small florets, stems finely diced

salt and pepper

Place the chicken in a clean tea towel and pat it dry. Transfer to a well greased slow cooker.

Melt the butter in a large glass jug in the microwave (or sit the jug in some hot water). Add the cream cheese and stir until it softens. Add the cream of celery soup and milk and stir until well combined.

Pour the cheese mixture over the chicken. Cover and cook on low for 4 hours. Remove the lid and sprinkle the broccoli florets and stems over the chicken. Cover and cook for 1 more hour. Season to taste. Serve with steamed brown rice.

Biscuits and sweet snacks

Most of the recipes in this section are good
for school lunchboxes or for after-school snacks.
Many are family favourites that have been made
for generations. When you're baking biscuits, you
don't need to go out and buy fancy 'cookie sheets'.
Baking trays are fine – they're usually about
26 cm × 35–40 cm and can fit a good dozen
or more bikkies on them – or you can
even use pizza trays.

Bulk biscuit recipe

This is the infamous recipe that started it all! When I first posted this on my blog in 2009, it used to be '120 biscuits for under $5', but prices have gone up a little. These are still really cheap (about $7) and easy to make, plus you get to make them any flavour you like. I've written out the recipe so that you can bake a batch and freeze the rest, but feel free to freeze the whole lot. This is a great way to cook fresh biscuits in 15 minutes when unexpected guests arrive!

Makes 120

500 g butter, softened

1 cup caster sugar

1 × 395 ml can sweetened condensed milk (see recipe page 99)

5 cups self-raising flour, sifted

2 tablespoons vanilla essence (optional)

additional flavourings (see next page)

Preheat the oven to 180°C. Line one or two baking trays with baking paper and set aside.

In a large mixing bowl, beat together the softened butter and caster sugar until light and fluffy. Add the condensed milk and mix well. Fold in the flour and mix until just combined. Take half (or a quarter) of the mixture and place in a separate bowl (or divide the mixture into four separate batches – whatever suits). Fold in the flavourings you want (see next page) to each batch of mixture.

To make a batch of biscuits now, with moist hands, roll teaspoonsful of the dough into balls and place on the prepared trays. Dip a fork in some flour and press down on each ball to flatten slightly. Bake for 10–15 minutes or until golden brown. Transfer to a cooling rack. Seal in an air-tight container for up to 1 week.

For the remaining dough, roll with your hands into a 20 cm long 'log' that is about 4 cm thick. Roll the log in baking paper and twist the ends to seal. Write the flavouring and the date on the outside and place in the freezer.

When you're ready to cook another batch, preheat the oven to 180°C, remove the frozen dough from the freezer and while still frozen, cut into 4 mm 'slices' or 'coins' of dough. Place the still-frozen dough onto a lined baking tray and cook for 15–20 minutes or until golden brown.

FLAVOUR OPTIONS

Most of these can simply be added in after the flour in any quantity up to about 1 cup, though how much you add will depend on whether you've divided your dough.

— Nutty: peanut butter, chopped macadamias, chopped walnuts, shredded coconut

— Fruity: sultanas, dried apricots, orange zest, lemon zest

— Spicy: nutmeg, cinnamon sugar

— Choc: chocolate bits, crushed smarties, malted milk powder

— Cereal crunch: cornflakes, rice bubbles

— Vanilla custard: substitute half of the flour for custard powder – they taste like yo-yos!

Coconut macaroons

This recipe is so simple even the kids can make it!

Makes about 36

⅔ cup (90 g) plain flour

½ teaspoon salt

1 × 395 ml can sweetened
condensed milk
(see recipe page 99)

1 teaspoon vanilla extract

3 cups (250 g) desiccated
coconut

Preheat the oven to 180°C and line a baking tray
with baking paper.

Sift the flour and salt together in a bowl. Add the
remaining ingredients and stir to make a thick
gloopy mixture.

Drop heaped teaspoonsful of the mixture onto
the baking paper (no need to worry about
spreading) and cook for 20 minutes, or until
golden. These will stay fresh for 7 days in a
sealed container in the fridge.

Cornflake biscuits

My grandma made the best cornflake biscuits in the whole world – and I'm lucky enough to have her original recipe! Just between you and me, sometimes I use chocolate bits instead of sultanas. Either way they're great!

Makes about 24

1½ cups cornflakes, lightly crushed

125 g butter

⅔ cup brown sugar

1 teaspoon vanilla extract

2 eggs

1¾ cups self-raising flour

1 cup sultanas

Preheat the oven to 180°C. Line two baking trays with baking paper and set aside.

Pour the crushed cornflakes onto a large plate and set aside.

Place the butter, sugar and vanilla in a bowl and, using a wooden spoon or an electric mixer, beat until pale and creamy. Add the eggs, one at a time, beating well after each addition until the mixture is smooth. Fold in the flour and sultanas, mixing until just combined.

Use your hands to roll tablespoonsful of the mixture in the cornflakes and place them on the prepared trays. Cook in batches for 18–20 minutes or until golden. Let the biscuits sit on the hot tray for 5 minutes before transferring them to a wire rack to cool completely. These will last for 7 days in a sealed container in the pantry.

Cheater's shortbread

This isn't your typical shortbread recipe, it's simpler but it tastes pretty damn close. (Traditional recipes often use rice flour which always ends up going mouldy in my pantry!)

Makes about 32

250 g butter

¾ cup icing sugar, sifted well

2½ cups plain flour, sifted

Preheat the oven to 150°C (a slow oven). Line one or two baking trays with baking paper and set aside.

Using a stand mixer (or a handheld electric mixer and bowl) whisk together the butter and icing sugar until light and fluffy. Turn your mixer to the lowest speed, add the sifted flour and mix until just combined.

Roll teaspoonful of dough into rough balls and place on the prepared trays. Use a floured fork to gently press down each biscuit. Bake for 20 minutes or until just starting to go golden. Allow the shortbread to cool on the tray before transferring to a cooling rack.

Nanna Darling's jam drops

This recipe is courtesy of our good friend Lydia's nanna. The biscuits are light and fluffy and the jam makes a deliciously gooey centre. A show-winning classic every cook should have!

Makes 12

110 g butter

¾ cup sugar

2 eggs

½ cup cornflour or custard powder

1¾ cups self-raising flour

½ cup good quality strawberry jam

Preheat the oven to 180°C. Line one or two baking trays with baking paper and set aside.

In a large mixing bowl, beat together the butter and sugar until light and fluffy. Add the eggs one at a time and beat until fluffy. Sift the cornflour or custard powder with the self-raising flour and fold into the creamed butter and sugar mixture.

Lightly flour your hands. The mixture should be tacky to touch. Roll heaped teaspoonsful of the mixture into balls and place on the prepared tray. Push a hole in the centre of each, using a finger (some people use thimbles!). Fill each with 1 teaspoon of jam. Bake for 8–10 minutes or until just starting to turn golden brown.

Hints & Tips

* You can use any type of jam – raspberry, apricot, cherry, even marmalade – as long as it's made with good-quality fruit.

* These can be stored in an airtight container in the pantry for up to 2 weeks, or in the freezer for up to 4 months.

Baked muesli bars

You'll never buy the processed ones after you taste these! Feel free to top with chocolate bits if you like, but I reckon you'll find these perfect as they are.

Makes about 16

2 cups rolled oats

¾ cup brown sugar

¾ cup dried apricots or dates, finely chopped

½ cup desiccated coconut

¼ cup rice bubbles

125 g butter

Preheat the oven to 180°C and line the base and sides of a 20 cm × 30 cm slice tin with baking paper.

Place all of the ingredients except the butter in a large bowl.

Melt the butter in a jug in the microwave and pour over the dry ingredients. Stir thoroughly until well combined. Press into the prepared tin. Bake for 25 minutes or until golden brown. Cut into bars while still nice and warm. Allow to cool in the tin for a while then transfer to a wire rack to cool completely – they'll be lovely and crunchy. These store well in a sealed container in the pantry for up to 10 days.

Honey rice bars

These are made with creamed honey, though they work equally well
with liquid honey.

Makes about 16

90 g butter

1 tablespoon creamed
honey

½ cup sugar

4 cups puffed rice (e.g.
Rice Bubbles)

Grease a 20 cm × 30 cm slice tin or line with
baking paper.

Place the puffed rice in a big mixing bowl and
set aside.

In a small saucepan, heat the butter, sugar and
honey over medium heat for 4–6 minutes or
until bubbling (be careful – the mixture spits!).
Pour the hot mixture into the puffed rice and mix
well. Press into the prepared tray and refrigerate
for 3–4 hours or until cold and firm. Cut into bars
and store in a sealed container in the fridge for
up to 1 week.

Pikelets

I do love a good fresh pikelet with golden syrup and cream! I'm not sure where this recipe came from, but it's the one I've always made, and it always turns out well. Simple and delicious!

Makes 8

1 teaspoon malt vinegar

1 cup milk

2 cups self-raising flour

1 teaspoon bicarbonate of soda

pinch of salt

¼ cup caster sugar

2 eggs at room temperature, whisked

2 tablespoons butter

Place the vinegar and milk in a small jug and set aside for 5 minutes to sour.

In a large bowl sift together the flour, bicarb soda and salt. Add the sugar and stir well to combine. Add the eggs and mix well. Slowly pour in the sour milk, whisking constantly, until the mixture forms a thick batter.

Heat a teaspoon of butter in a large frying pan over medium heat until sizzling. Place ¼ cup of batter in the pan (you may be able to fit two or more at once) and cook for 5–6 minutes, or until bubbles form on the top and the outside edge has set. Flip and cook for another 2–3 minutes. Repeat until all the batter is cooked, adding a teaspoon of butter to the pan before each batch.

Serve with butter and jam or fresh fruit and whipped cream – anything you like! These will keep in a sealed container in the fridge for 3 days.

Muesli slice

These are great for school lunches as they don't contain nuts, plus they are free of gluten and dairy. And you don't even have to turn the oven on!

Makes 18

1 cup rolled oats

1 cup desiccated coconut

½ cup sunflower seeds

125 g butter

125 g honey (or golden syrup or rice malt syrup)

½ cup dates, finely chopped

½ teaspoon salt

½ teaspoon cinnamon (or ¼ teaspoon each of cinnamon and nutmeg)

Grease a 20 cm × 30 cm slice tin (or line it with baking paper).

Place the oats, coconut and sunflower seeds in a frying pan over medium heat and toast lightly for 2–3 minutes until fragrant. Pour into a bowl and allow to cool.

Return the pan to the heat with the butter, honey or syrup, dates, salt and spices and heat until the mixture comes together and starts to bubble. Pour over the dry ingredients and mix well.

Press into the prepared tin and refrigerate overnight. Cut into squares and enjoy! These will keep in a sealed container in the fridge for 5 days.

Apple and oat muffins

The oats give these muffins a lovely texture. They're not too sugary, either, which is great if you're trying to cut down. Perfect for school lunchboxes.

Makes 12

1 cup rolled oats

1 cup buttermilk
(see recipe page 63)

1 cup wholemeal plain flour

1 teaspoon baking powder

1 teaspoon bicarbonate of soda

½ cup brown sugar

½ cup apple puree

1 egg

Place the rolled oats and milk in a large bowl and leave to stand for 2 hours at room temperature.

Preheat the oven to 180°C. Grease a 12-cup muffin tray or line it with paper cases.

Add the remaining ingredients to the oat mixture and stir until thoroughly combined. Spoon into the muffin cups. Bake for 30 minutes or until just cooked and a skewer inserted in the centre comes out clean. Store in a sealed container in the pantry for 3 days. These also freeze well for 1 month.

Two-ingredient fruit salad cupcakes

This is one of the easiest and cheapest recipes around if you buy generic-brand ingredients.

Makes 12

1 × 570 g packet vanilla or butter cake mix

1 × 440 g can fruit salad

Preheat the oven to 200°C. Line a 12-cup muffin tray with paper cases, or use a silicon cupcake tray.

In a bowl, mix together the cake mix and the fruit salad (including the juice) and spoon evenly into the cupcake cases or tray. Bake for 20 minutes or until golden. Delicious served with cream and ice cream or iced with orange icing.

Hints & Tips

* Instead of cake mix you can use 2 cups of self-raising flour and 1 cup of sugar.

* You can also make this as a cake. Grease a round cake tin and cut baking paper to fit the base. Pour in the mixture and bake for 45 minutes or until cooked through.

* If your cupcakes or cake have 'soggy bottoms', just flip them upside down and pop back in the oven for a few minutes.

Cakes and slices

When I was living on $50 a week,
I quite often picked up generic-brand packet
cake mixes to make cupcakes for the kids. At less
than a dollar each, and with eggs being free from my
neighbour, it was a truly frugal option. Now, I have to
confess that I've found a few tricks to make packet
cakes taste 'gourmet'. (I often made them for work
and the girls raved about them – not realising they
were from a packet!) Here's what you do:

– Add an extra egg

– Replace the oil with melted butter

– Add a teaspoon of vanilla extract

– Replace any water in the instructions with milk

So, shhh! That's our little secret.

Five-cup fruit loaf

This fruit loaf is made from easy staple items you will find in your pantry, so you won't have to leave the house to buy ingredients. Yep, that's right, no bra and pants needed. Or else it isn't happening today!

Makes 10–12 slices

1 cup rolled oats

1 cup self-raising flour

1 cup brown sugar

1 cup dried fruit (any kind, such as sultanas, currants, raisins, dates, dried apricots)

1 cup milk

Preheat the oven to 160°C. Grease a 21 cm × 11 cm loaf tin and line the base with baking paper.

In a large bowl, mix together all the dry ingredients. Make a well in the centre and add the milk. Mix well with a wooden spoon and pour into the prepared tin.

Bake for 45 minutes or until a skewer inserted in the centre comes out clean.

Slice and serve warm with butter. Store in a tin or well-sealed container. These will last 3 days if stored in the cupboard, 1 week in the fridge, or 2 months in the freezer.

Frugal chocolate cake

Everyone needs a go-to chocolate cake recipe, and here's the one I use.

Serves 8

2 cups self-raising flour

⅔ cup white sugar

2 tablespoons cocoa

125 g butter, melted and cooled

2 large eggs, at room temperature

¾ cup milk

Preheat the oven to 180°C. Grease a 22 cm round cake tin (or a 12-cup muffin tray).

Place the flour, sugar and cocoa in a large mixing bowl.

In another bowl, whisk together the butter and eggs. Add the milk slowly, whisking well.

Add the wet ingredients to the dry ingredients and mix well. Transfer the mixture to the prepared tin or tray and bake the cake for 40 minutes or the muffins for 15–20 minutes or until a skewer inserted in the centre comes out clean.

Three-ingredient fruit cake

Even nanna will be impressed with this super easy fruit cake! I've also given you another option if you don't want to soak the fruit overnight.

Serves 8

600 g mixed dried fruit

2½ cups milk

2 cups self-raising flour, sifted

Place the dried fruit and milk in a large bowl and cover with plastic wrap. Refrigerate overnight.

Preheat the oven to 160°C and grease a 22 cm round cake tin.

Remove the soaked fruit from the fridge and fold in the flour. Pour into the prepared tin and bake for 1 hour, or until a skewer inserted in the centre comes out clean. Allow to cool in the tin for 30 minutes before turning out onto a wire rack. Serve cold sliced with butter, or warm with whipped cream.

This cake will keep in the pantry for 7 days, or in the freezer for 3 months (place baking paper between slices in a zip-lock bag).

Hints & Tips

✳ To make a **Quick Fruitcake**, preheat the oven to 180°C. In a large bowl mix together 1 kg mixed dried fruit, 2 cups of fruit juice and 2 cups of self-raising flour. Pour into a greased and lined 22 cm round cake tin and bake for 90 minutes. Turn off the heat and leave the cake in the oven for an additional 30 minutes

Frugal chocolate mud cake

I adore chocolate mud cake, but many recipes use chocolate bars, which makes them super expensive. My version uses cocoa, which is much more economical – and you would never know!

Serves 8

½ cup cocoa (heaped)

1½ cups plain flour

1 teaspoon bicarbonate of soda

125 g butter

1½ cups caster sugar

2 eggs

icing sugar, for dusting

Preheat the oven to 180°C. Grease a 20 cm cake tin (round or square) and set aside.

Sift the cocoa into a jug. Add 1 cup of water, stir well and set aside.

Sift the flour and bicarb soda into a small bowl and set aside.

Beat together the butter and sugar until light and fluffy (use a wooden spoon or a handheld electric mixer). Add the eggs, one at a time, beating well between each addition. Add the cocoa mixture bit by bit, alternating with the flour, beating well between additions until the ingredients are well combined. Pour into the prepared tin and bake for 1 hour. Allow the cake to cool in the tin for 5 minutes before turning out onto a wire rack to cool completely. Dust with icing sugar.

White coconut cake

This is perhaps one of the easiest cakes to make – and no eggs!

Makes about 10 slices

1 cup shredded or desiccated coconut

1 cup self-raising flour

½ cup caster sugar

1 cup milk

icing sugar, sifted, for dusting

Preheat the oven to 180°C and grease a 20 cm × 10 cm loaf tin.

Place all the ingredients in a mixing bowl and whisk until combined (don't over-mix). Pour into the prepared tin and bake for 45 minutes or until a skewer inserted in the centre comes out clean. Dust with icing sugar and enjoy!

Whole orange cake

There's nothing so scrumptious as a flourless orange cake, but they cost a fortune to make because almond meal is so expensive. This version has the same delicious flavour, but without the bank-breaking almond meal.

Serves 8

1 large orange, cut into chunks

180 g butter, melted

3 eggs, beaten

1 cup caster sugar

1½ cups self-raising flour

Preheat the oven to 180°C. Grease a 22 cm round cake tin and set aside.

Fill a small saucepan with water and heat until boiling. Add the whole orange (do not cut it up), cover and simmer for 1 hour. Drain.

Place the orange in a food processor (skin, seeds and all) and process to a smooth puree. Pour the orange puree into a bowl. Add the butter, eggs and caster sugar and mix well. Fold in the flour.

Pour the mixture into the prepared tin and bake for 40 minutes. Cool in the tin for 10 minutes before turning out onto a wire rack to cool completely.

Hints & Tips

✳ For an even stronger citrus flavour, while the cake is still hot, poke a few holes in the top, and pour over ½ cup of fresh orange or lemon juice. Leave it to cool.

Frugal date loaf

This recipe was sent in to us from Dana Butterworth in Bundaberg. Thanks, Dana. We think this recipe rocks!

Makes 10–12 slices

4 breakfast wheat biscuits, crushed (Weet-Bix, VitaBrits or generic)

1 cup dates, pitted and chopped

¾ cup caster sugar

1 teaspoon bicarbonate of soda

1 cup boiling water

2 eggs, beaten

1 cup self-raising flour

Preheat the oven to 180°C and grease a 21 cm × 11 cm loaf tin.

In a large bowl place the wheat biscuits, dates, sugar, bicarb soda and boiling water. Stir well and leave to sit for 10–15 minutes to allow the biscuits to soak up the liquid.

When the wheat mixture has thickened, stir in the eggs and self-raising flour and mix until well combined. Transfer to the prepared loaf tin and bake for 45 minutes. Cool in the tin for 5 minutes before turning out onto a wire rack. Slice and spread with butter.

Eligh's caramelised banana bread

Who is Eligh you might ask? Well Eligh is the son of a very good friend of mine – he was about 13 when he came up with this recipe all on his own. It is honestly the *best* banana bread I have tasted. If ever I had a day I was feeling a little down, Lydia (Eligh's mum) would whip up this cake with a little cinnamon butter to go on top. Makes you feel good from the inside out.

Makes 10–12 slices

3 overripe bananas

3 teaspoons bicarbonate of soda

1 cup raw sugar

1 tiny pinch of salt

2 eggs, lightly beaten

¼ cup canola oil or melted butter

1½ cups plain flour, sifted well

½ cup buttermilk (see recipe page 63)

Preheat the oven to 130°C (very slow). Line a 21 cm × 11 cm loaf tin with aluminium foil and set aside.

Mash the bananas in a mixing bowl. Add the bicarb soda, sugar and salt and mix well. Stir in the eggs and then the oil or butter, mixing well between each addition. Fold in the flour then add the buttermilk, stirring until thoroughly combined.

Pour the batter into the prepared loaf tin and bake for 2 hours or until a skewer inserted in the centre comes out clean. Allow to cool in the tin for at least 10 minutes, then take the whole loaf out including the foil.

Hints & Tips

✳ The secret to the delicious richness of this cake is that it is cooked at a lower temperature for longer. Don't be tempted to rush it.

✳ Keep the loaf in a sealed container in the fridge for up to 6 days

Bran tea cake

A great way to amp up your fibre!

Makes about 10 slices

1 cup bran cereal

1 cup self-raising flour

½ cup dried fruit

½ cup brown sugar

1 cup milk

Preheat the oven to 180°C and grease a 20 cm × 10 cm loaf tin.

In a large mixing bowl, combine all of the ingredients and mix well. Pour into the prepared tin and bake for 45 minutes or until a skewer inserted in the centre comes out clean.

Sand cake

If a sponge cake and a butter cake had a baby, the result would be a sand cake. I love this cake – it is so easy to make – you literally throw everything in, mix and bake. I like to make double and triple batches as the cake freezes really well. It also makes for a great birthday cake because it is 'heavy' enough to withstand fondant.

Serves 8

1 cup self-raising flour

1 tablespoon cornflour or custard powder

125 g butter, room temperature

¾ cup caster sugar

¼ cup milk

2 eggs

Preheat the oven to 180°C. Grease a 22 cm round cake tin with butter and dust with flour.

Place all of the ingredients in a large bowl and beat for 6 minutes or until pale and creamy (use a stand mixer if you have one). Spread evenly into the prepared tin and bake for 35–40 minutes or until a skewer inserted into the centre comes out clean. Leave to cool for 5 minutes before turning out onto a wire rack to cool completely.

Hints & Tips

✳ To freeze, wrap the cooked cake in a double layer of plastic wrap. Place on a flat surface in the freezer – it will keep well for up to 2 months.

Traditional Weet-Bix slice

These are so delicious! I know I use Weet-Bix a lot, but it's a cereal with a lot more fibre and a lot less sugar than any other (apart from oats). There are generic versions, too, which are cheaper.

Makes 12–15

3 Weet-Bix

1 cup self-raising flour

¾ cup brown sugar

1 cup shredded coconut

150 g butter

2 tablespoons peanut butter

LEMON GLAZE

2 teaspoons lemon juice

½ cup icing sugar

Preheat the oven to 180°C. Grease a 20 cm × 30 cm slice tin and line with baking paper.

In a bowl, crush the Weet-Bix then stir in the flour, sugar and coconut.

Place the butter and peanut butter in small microwave-proof jug. Microwave in 30 second increments, until melted. Pour into the dry ingredients and mix well. Press the mixture into the prepared tin and bake for 15 minutes. Allow to cool in the tin.

Meanwhile, mix the lemon juice and icing sugar together in a cup and stir until smooth. When the slice is cool, drizzle the lemon icing over the top.

Hints & Tips

* Keep the slice in the fridge or it will become very crumbly. Also, it's not suitable for freezing.

Frugal chocolate slice

This yummy slice is made from basic, staple ingredients – and is a good one for the lunchbox!

Makes 12–15

1 cup self-raising flour

¾ cup brown sugar

1 tablespoon cocoa

1 cup puffed rice or Rice Bubbles

125 g butter, melted

CHOCOLATE ICING

1 cup icing sugar

1 tablespoon cocoa

1 tablespoon butter

desiccated coconut, for sprinkling

Preheat the oven to 180°C and grease a 20 cm × 30 cm slice tin.

Place the flour, sugar, cocoa and puffed rice in a mixing bowl and stir until well combined. Pour in the melted butter and mix well. Press into the prepared tin and bake for 10 minutes. Remove from the oven and leave to cool slightly.

Meanwhile, combine the ingredients for the icing in a small bowl and stir until smooth. While the slice is still warm, spread the chocolate icing evenly over the top and sprinkle with coconut. Store in a sealed container in the fridge for 5 days.

Apple and sour cream slice

This recipe has been around forever, but it is still a favourite – and so easy. I always make this when I have to open my carton of sour cream – it's a great way to use it up before it goes manky.

Serves 8

1 × 545 g packet butter or vanilla cake mix

1 cup desiccated coconut

125 g butter, melted

1 × 400 g can cooked apple slices

300 g sour cream

1 teaspoon cinnamon

1 teaspoon caster sugar

Preheat the oven to 180°C. Grease a 20 cm square cake tin and line well with baking paper.

In a bowl, combine the cake mix, coconut and melted butter and mix well. Spoon into the prepared tin and press evenly. Cook for 15 minutes or until lightly browned. Remove from the oven and allow to cool slightly.

Spread the apple over the base and then pour over the sour cream. Sprinkle the top with the cinnamon and sugar. Return to the oven for a further 20 minutes or until the sour cream is set.

Town bike slice

This great recipe is cheap, easy, and everyone loves it – hence the name!
Thank you to my good friend Donna Faithful for giving me this recipe.

Makes 12–15

1 cup chocolate bits

1 cup desiccated coconut

1 cup chopped nuts
(any kind)

1 cup puffed rice (Rice
Bubbles or Coco Pops)

1 × 395 ml can sweetened
condensed milk (see
recipe page 99)

Preheat the oven to 180°C and line a 20 cm ×
30 cm slice tin with baking paper.

Spread the chocolate bits evenly over the base of
the prepared tin. Sprinkle over the cup of coconut
as evenly as possible, followed by the nuts, puffed
rice and lastly the condensed milk. There's no
need to mix it up – just add each ingredient as
a new layer.

Bake for 20 minutes, remove from the oven
and leave to cool (it will be sticky to touch).
When cold, slice into squares. Store in a sealed
container in the pantry for up to 5 days.

Slow-cooker chocolate fudge

Fudge is a decadent treat, but can be quite fussy to make. This very naughty version is way simpler and only has two ingredients!

Serves 6

500 g chocolate bits

1 × 395 ml can sweetened condensed milk (see recipe page 99)

Line the base and sides of the slow cooker with baking paper.

Pour the chocolate bits and condensed milk into the slow cooker. Cook on low for 4 hours, stirring well every hour so that the edges do not burn.

When cooked, use the baking paper to remove the fudge from the slow cooker. It should hold its shape but will still be very sticky and 'bendy'. Place on a tray (still on the baking paper) and pop in the fridge for 4 hours to set. When firm, cut into squares and enjoy.

No-bake peanut butter and oat slice

With only three ingredients and no baking required, this is a good one for the kids to make.

Makes 16

3 cups rolled oats

1 cup peanut butter (not the natural stuff – it is too oily)

½ cup honey

Line a 20 cm square cake tin with baking paper.

In a microwave-proof bowl, melt the peanut butter and honey in the microwave in 30 second increments until it is easy to pour. Mix it into the oats and combine well. Press into the lined tin and place in the fridge until set. Cut into squares.

Easy date slice

Dates are naturally sweet, so feel free to reduce the amount of sugar in this recipe, though brown sugar does add a delicious caramel flavour!

Makes 12–15

1 dried dates, pitted and chopped

90 g butter

1 cup brown sugar

1 egg

1½ cups self-raising flour, sifted

Preheat the oven to 180°C and grease a 20 cm square cake tin with baking paper.

Place the dates in a food processor and process to a chunky paste (like lumpy jam).

Using an electric mixer, beat the butter until light and creamy. Add the sugar and beat again. Whisk in the egg. Gently fold in the sifted flour and creamed dates. Press into the prepared tin and bake for 20 minutes or until golden. Cut into squares and enjoy with some double cream and a cup of tea!

Hints & Tips

* If you don't like dates, you can substitute them with pretty much any dried fruit. Dried apple and dried apricots work well.

Passionfruit cheesecake slice

This is a good one to take to a friend's place for a special morning or afternoon tea.

Makes 24

BASE

1 cup self-raising flour

1 cup shredded coconut

½ cup caster sugar

125 g butter, melted

FILLING

125 g cream cheese, room temperature

1 × 395 ml can sweetened condensed milk (see recipe page 99)

juice of 1 lemon

pulp of 1 passionfruit

Preheat the oven to 180°C and line a 20 cm × 30 cm slice tin with baking paper.

To make the base, place all of the ingredients in a mixing bowl, and stir until well combined. Press into the base of the prepared tin, making sure you get right into the corners. Flatten with the back of a spoon. Bake for 15 minutes or until golden. Remove from the oven and allow to cool in the tin.

To make the filling, place the cream cheese in a bowl and beat with an electric mixer until very smooth. Add the condensed milk and beat until well combined. Stir in the lemon juice and passionfruit pulp. Pour the filling over the base and smooth the top. Place in the fridge until set (about 4 hours or overnight). Cut into 5 cm squares.

Leftover cereal bars

This is a great way to use up all the little bits of cereal left in the bottom of bags.

Makes 15

4 cups cereal (any kind)

½ cup brown sugar

½ cup desiccated coconut

125 g butter

3 tablespoons honey

1 tablespoon golden syrup

½ cup chocolate bits (optional)

Preheat the oven to 180°C and line a 20 cm × 30 cm slice tin with baking paper.

Place the cereal, sugar and coconut in a bowl and stir well with a wooden spoon until well combined.

Place the butter, honey and golden syrup in a small microwave-proof jug. Microwave in 30 second bursts until melted. Pour into the dry ingredients and mix well. Press the mixture into the prepared tin and top with chocolate bits (if desired). Bake for 20 minutes or until golden brown. Allow to cool before cutting into bars.

To store, place in a sealed container in the fridge for up to 6 days.

Desserts

When it comes to reducing your weekly grocery bills, desserts are definitely where you can save money. Yet they are nice to have now and then. Here are some super cheap and easy recipes that won't break the bank.

Homemade chocolate pudding

Our kids love this dessert, and the great thing is that you can reduce the sugar without affecting the recipe. Plus, if you freeze this mixture in paper cups and add a paddle pop stick you get really yummy homemade chocolate ice blocks!

Serves 6

⅓ cup cocoa

⅓ cup cornflour

½ cup caster sugar

800 ml milk

In a small bowl, sift the cocoa, cornflour and caster sugar together. Add 300 ml of the milk and mix well.

Place the remaining 500 ml of milk in a saucepan over medium heat. When it starts to steam, take off the heat and whisk in the cocoa mixture. Reduce the heat to low. Return the saucepan to the heat and continue to whisk for 5 minutes or until the mixture thickens. Allow to cool slightly.

Pour into a serving bowl, or six ramekins, and cover with plastic wrap – making sure the wrap touches the top of the mixture (so a skin doesn't form). Pop it in the fridge for 2 hours or until it is cold.

Chocolate mug cake

Older kids love to make these as there is no fussing with ovens or hot plates. Just make sure they use tea towels or oven mitts to take the mugs out of the microwave.

Serves 2

⅓ cup self-raising flour

⅓ cup sugar

2 tablespoons cocoa

¼ cup chocolate bits

1 egg

¼ cup milk

¼ cup canola oil or melted butter

¾ cup boiling water

Place the flour, sugar, cocoa and chocolate bits in a jug and mix well. Add the egg, milk and oil or butter and mix until well combined. Stir in the boiling water and mix again. Pour the mixture evenly into two microwave-proof mugs.

Microwave each one on high for 2 minutes, or until the cake is cooked (it may take another 30 seconds or so, depending on your microwave). Top with a dollop of cream or ice cream and enjoy!

Choc hazelnut mug cake

This moist, delicious cake needs a very large mug, or it will spill over the top and make a mess!

Serves 2

⅓ cup self-raising flour

⅓ cup sugar

1 egg

¼ cup cocoa

¼ cup chocolate hazelnut spread (e.g. Nutella)

¼ cup milk

¼ cup canola oil

Place all of the ingredients in a jug and whisk well with a fork until the mixture is nice and smooth. Pour into two microwave-proof mugs and microwave on high for 2 minutes or until just cooked. Top with whipped cream or ice cream.

Apple crumble charlotte

My mum often served this dessert with lashings of freshly made custard. So to me, this is more of a pudding than a cake.

Serves 6

1 × 400 g can cooked apple slices ('pie apples')

¼ cup brown sugar

½ cup rolled oats

2 tablespoons butter, melted

1 × 570 g packet vanilla or butter cake mix

1 egg

½ cup milk

Preheat the oven to 180°C. Grease a 24 cm pie dish and line the base with baking paper.

In a small bowl, mix together the apple, sugar and oats. Add 1 tablespoon of the butter and mix until well combined. Spread the apple mixture over the base of the prepared dish.

Make up the cake mix according to the instructions (with egg, milk and remaining butter) and pour the batter over the top of the apple mixture. Bake for 35 minutes or until the cake is cooked through. Serve warm with cream and ice cream.

Real vanilla custard

It might seem easier to buy custard in a carton, but it is actually way cheaper to make it yourself, and so much healthier, too.

Serves 2

2 egg yolks

2 teaspoons cornflour

1 tablespoon sugar

1 cup milk

½ teaspoon vanilla extract

In a large jug, whisk together the egg yolks, cornflour and sugar until well combined. Set aside.

Heat the milk and vanilla in a saucepan over low heat until just warm (not hot). Remove from the heat and carefully pour into the jug with the egg mixture.

Now pour the milk and egg mixture back into the saucepan and return it to medium heat, whisking constantly until boiling. Take off the heat and whisk until the custard is thick enough to coat the back of a spoon. (If the mixture is not thickening, gently heat it again.)

Serve hot or cold. If serving cold, add a layer of plastic wrap to the surface of the custard as it cools to prevent a skin forming.

Coconut impossible pie

Like other 'impossible' recipes, you literally just mix everything together and throw it in the oven! And this one is so delicious I'm going to the kitchen to make it right now!

Serves 6

1 cup desiccated coconut

1 cup plain flour

1 cup caster sugar

2 teaspoons vanilla extract

4 eggs, whisked

100 g butter, melted

3 cups milk

Preheat the oven to 180°C and grease a large pie dish.

Throw all the ingredients together in a bowl and mix until well combined. Pour into the prepared dish and bake for 1 hour. Allow to cool slightly before slicing and serving warm with ice cream.

Creamy rice pudding

Probably one of my favourite frugal desserts of all time, this is delicious hot or cold. I've given instructions for cooking it on the stove, but you can also use the microwave.

Serves 6

1 cup rice (any type, but I like arborio)

pinch of salt

¾ cup sugar

¼ cup cornflour

3 cups milk

2 eggs

1 tablespoon butter

2 teaspoons vanilla essence

½ cup raisins (optional)

pinch of cinnamon or nutmeg

Place the rice, salt and 2 cups of water in a saucepan over medium heat. Cover and bring to the boil. Reduce the heat to very low and cook for 15–20 minutes or until the water is absorbed. Remove from the heat and set it aside.

In another saucepan, mix the sugar and cornflour with ¼ cup of the milk and stir to make a paste. Place over medium heat and whisk in the remaining milk. Continue whisking until the mixture is hot and starts to thicken (about 5 minutes). Reduce the heat to low and remove the pan from the heat.

Beat the eggs in a bowl. Scoop 1 cup of the hot milk mixture and pour it slowly into the eggs, whisking constantly so the eggs don't curdle. Now pour the egg mixture back into the hot milk mixture to create a custard. Return the pan to the heat and cook until nearly bubbling (do not boil). Remove from the heat. Stir through the butter and vanilla. Add the cooked rice and raisins (if using), stirring gently. Sprinkle over the cinnamon or nutmeg and serve.

Jelly whip

Sometimes called 'flummery', this super-sweet dessert has just two ingredients and costs next to nothing.

Serves 4

1 × 375 g can evaporated milk (refrigerated)

1 × 85 g packet jelly crystals (any flavour)

Make up the jelly in a jug according to the instructions on the packet but using *half* of the recommended amount of water. Refrigerate for 1–2 hours or until almost set but still a bit runny and wobbly.

Pour the cold evaporated milk into a bowl and use an electric mixer to beat it for 2 minutes or until it triples in size and is really thick. While still whisking the milk, slowly add the jelly mixture. Once the mixture is well combined, give the sides of the bowl a good scrape down (so you don't miss any crystals) and give it one last whisk. Pour the mixture into four glasses. Refrigerate for 1 hour before serving.

Slow-cooker bread and butter pudding

Frugal cooks have been making bread and butter pudding for centuries (literally!). It was a great way to use stale, leftover bread in the days before freezers, and is still a popular dish.

Serves 6

4 slices of raisin toast
or extra thick fruit bread
(or 8 slices standard size)

2 cups milk

4 eggs

¼ cup sugar

1 teaspoon vanilla extract

½ cup sultanas or mixed
dried fruit

¼ teaspoon nutmeg

canola oil spray

Line the slow cooker with baking paper and give it a good spray with canola oil. Cut the bread into triangles and use to line the bottom of the slow cooker.

In a jug, beat together the milk, eggs, sugar and vanilla until smooth. Carefully pour the egg and milk mixture over the fruit bread. Sprinkle the sultanas or dried fruit and nutmeg on top.

Cover and cook on low for 3–4 hours. Serve warm with ice cream.

Condensed milk ice cream

Once you try homemade ice cream, it is pretty hard to go back to the shop-bought stuff. The only difference is that homemade ice cream is often harder to scoop out. To avoid this (yes, there is a remedy), keep your homemade ice cream in a container then place the container in a large zip-lock bag – it will always be 'scoop-able'.

Serves 4

600 ml cream

1 teaspoon vanilla extract

1 × 395 ml can sweetened condensed milk (see recipe page 99)

Beat the cream with an electric beater until it begins to thicken (about 4–5 minutes). Add the vanilla extract and continue beating until the mixture is very thick and light. Gradually add the condensed milk, beating continuously until it thickens to a nice creamy consistency.

Pour the mixture into a container and freeze for 6 hours or until almost firm.

Remove from the freezer, beat the mixture again until light, and then re-freeze. Enjoy how good it is!

Dairy-free raspberry ice cream

Many people who give up dairy foods say that they miss ice cream the most. And until recently, I didn't even know that it was possible to make ice cream without milk products! This tastes just like soft serve, only better. Recipe by Kate Carlile from Gympie.

Serves 4

500 g frozen raspberries
(see tip below)

¼ cup caster sugar

2 egg whites

mint sprigs, to serve

Place the frozen raspberries and sugar in a blender and blitz for about 1 minute, or until the mixture is smooth. Transfer to a mixing bowl.

In another bowl, whip the egg whites with an electric mixer until stiff peaks form. Fold the egg whites into the raspberry mixture. Spoon into dessert cups and serve immediately with mint sprigs. Alternatively, seal in a container and freeze until ready to use.

Hints & Tips

✳ Other fruits that work well include frozen bananas (peel them first!), frozen mango (deseeded, peeled and chopped before freezing), or frozen blueberries or strawberries.

Slow-cooker cinnamon scrolls

Scrolls in the slow cooker? You better believe it! The slow cooker is great for baking – it almost 'steams' your delectable dessert. Plus it beats having to turn on an oven.

Makes 8–9

3 cups self-raising flour

1 teaspoon cinnamon

½ teaspoon bicarbonate of soda

1 teaspoon salt

2 tablespoons caster sugar

100 g butter, room temperature

1¼ cups milk

FILLING

½ cup walnuts

½ cup brown sugar

½ teaspoon cinnamon

Set your slow cooker to high and let it preheat for about 20 minutes. Place a sheet of baking paper in the base of the insert so that it reaches up the sides a bit (this helps you get the scrolls out).

In a bowl sift together the flour, cinnamon, bicarb soda and salt. Stir in the caster sugar. Add the butter and rub it in with your fingertips until the mixture resembles breadcrumbs. Pour in the milk and use a butter knife to combine (don't over-mix). Gently knead the mixture to make a rough dough. Turn out onto a floured surface and use a rolling pin to press into a rectangular shape about 30 cm × 20 cm and 3–4 cm thick.

To make the filling, crush the walnuts in a mini food processor so they are crumbly but not turned to dust. Pour into a small bowl and mix with the brown sugar and cinnamon. Pour half of the filling over the dough, and then roll it up from the shortest side. Cut the dough into 8–9 scrolls and gently arrange them on the bottom of the slow cooker with the cut side facing up. Pour over the remaining walnut and sugar mixture. Place a tea towel over the opening of the slow cooker before fitting the lid. (This stops condensation from dripping on the scrolls and making them soggy.) Cook for 90 minutes. Store in sealed container in the pantry for up to 3 days.

Tropical trifle

This is a simple and frugal take on the traditional trifle. It's perfect for Christmas Day when lots of tropical fruits are in season! Although this looks beautiful in a proper trifle bowl, you can simply use a 20 cm clear glass bowl and it's just as good.

Serves 12

1 × 85 g packet orange jelly crystals

1 × 85 g packet mango jelly crystals

1 × large packet vanilla cake mix

2 eggs

1 cup milk

2 tablespoons butter, melted

1 × 600 ml carton of thick custard (or make your own, see page 306)

500 ml thickened cream

300 ml double cream

2 fresh mangoes

1 × 125 g can pineapple rings, drained (or fresh pineapple)

Make the jellies according to the packet directions and place in the fridge for 1–2 hours.

Make the vanilla cake according to the packet directions (with eggs, milk and melted butter) and allow to cool.

Cut the cake into 3 cm squares and place half around the bottom of a 20 cm trifle bowl, ensuring that all gaps are filled. Pour over half the custard and spread evenly with a spoon. Spoon half the orange jelly and half the mango jelly over the custard. Pour over ¾ of the thickened cream, spreading out evenly.

Slice the fresh mangoes on either side of the seed and score each half with cross-hatch cuts (don't cut through the skin). Now push up the skin to 'pop' out the mango cubes, running a paring knife under the cubes to separate them from the skin. Peel and slice the mango flesh from around the seed. (This is your cue to suck on the mango seed!) Place a layer of mango on top of the cream, reserving the cubes from one mango cheek. Top the mango with the remaining custard.

Lay the pineapple rings in a single layer on top of the custard. Top with the remaining jellies in the centre, and then the mango on top of the jelly. Dollop remaining cream around outside of the jelly for decoration. Refrigerate until just before serving.

Condensed milk tart

This is perhaps the easiest dessert to make in the history of the world. It is like a cheesecake – but has no cheese! To save even more dollars, you can make the pastry yourself (page 93), but to keep things easy we are just using a pre-baked pastry shell available from most supermarkets. Recipe by Barbara Allen from Cecil Plains.

Serves 6

1 × 395 ml can sweetened condensed milk (see recipe page 99)

juice of 1 lemon

1 × 150 g shortcrust flan shell.

Pour the condensed milk and juice into a bowl and mix until it lightens in colour and thickens (should happen pretty much as soon as it is all combined). Pour into the pastry shell and refrigerate until chilled. Serve with fresh fruit.

Chocolate self-saucing pudding

My good friend Shelley gave me this recipe – it's so much better than the packet variety, and so easy to make! Recipe by Shelley Gilbert from Gympie.

Serves 4

PUDDING

1 cup self-raising flour

2 tablespoons cocoa, well sifted

½ cup sugar

1 egg

½ cup milk

2 tablespoons butter, melted

1 teaspoon vanilla extract

SAUCE

¾ cup brown sugar

⅓ cup cocoa

2½ cups boiling water

Preheat the oven to 170°C. Grease a 20 cm round casserole dish with butter.

Sift the flour and cocoa into a bowl then stir in the sugar. Set aside.

In a jug, whisk the egg with the milk, butter and vanilla. Gradually add to the dry ingredients, stirring until just combined but not over-mixed. Pour into the prepared dish.

In another jug, whisk together the sauce ingredients until smooth. Pour the sauce slowly over the back of a large spoon into the dish (this prevents the pudding mixture from being disturbed). Bake for 35 minutes or until the pudding is cooked and the sauce nice and gooey. Serve with vanilla ice cream.

Slow-cooker creamy coconut rice

This recipe came about after I had too many tins of coconut-flavoured evaporated milk in my cupboard and decided to experiment. It does have a few naughties in there, but dessert is just a sometimes food.

Serves 4

1 × 400 ml can coconut flavoured evaporated milk

1 cup arborio rice

1 × 395 ml can condensed milk

1 litre milk

Set the slow cooker to low. Add the evaporated milk, rice, condensed milk and 250 ml of the milk. Put the lid on. Cook for 3 hours, stirring every 30 minutes for the first 2 hours, then every 15 minutes thereafter, adding more milk as the rice absorbs it. Once all the milk is added and the rice is cooked through (the mixture will be nice and thick), turn off the heat.

Serve warm or cold.

Hints & Tips

✳ You may need to add more milk – all slow cookers cook differently.

Lemon jelly cheesecake mousse

This is my Jelly Whip recipe taken to the next level. Very more-ish!

Serves 4

1 × 85 g packet lemon jelly crystals

½ cup boiling water

1 × 250 g packet cream cheese, softened

250 ml thickened cream

Place the jelly crystals in a jug with the boiling water. Stir constantly until the crystals have dissolved. Allow to cool to room temperature.

When cooled, transfer to a blender with the cream cheese and ½ cup cold water. Blend until the mixture is smooth. Fold in the thickened cream and pour into four glasses (or a 20 cm trifle bowl). Refrigerate for 5 hours or overnight.

Butter caramel self-saucing pudding

This is another recipe submitted by mother of three and brilliant cook, Cassie Billingsley. Thanks Cassie!

Serves 4

1 cup self-raising flour

1¼ cups brown sugar (dark brown sugar if you can get it)

60 g butter, melted, plus 3 teaspoons extra

1 egg, lightly beaten

½ cup milk

1 cup boiling water

Preheat the oven to 180°C and grease a small high-sided cake tin (about 15 cm diameter).

Sift the flour and ½ cup of the brown sugar into a bowl. Add the melted butter and mix. Add the egg and milk and gently whisk to make a batter (don't over-mix). Pour the batter into the prepared tin.

In a separate bowl, place the remaining brown sugar and boiling water and stir until the sugar has dissolved. Carefully pour the hot sugar mixture over the batter, using the back of a spoon to disperse the mixture well. Dollop the 3 teaspoons of butter over the top and bake for 20 minutes or until the pudding has risen and is golden on top. Serve with all things naughty – ice cream, cream and custard!

Old-fashioned steamed pudding

This is just like Nanna used to make – soft, warm and delectable. The only problem with steamed puddings is that they need to be eaten within 24 hours as they spoil very quickly – luckily they're so yummy, we never have a problem finishing them!

Serves 4–6

40 g butter

½ cup caster sugar

2 eggs

2 cups self-raising flour

pinch salt

1¼ cups milk

¾ cup jam, golden syrup or chocolate sauce

In a large bowl, use an electric mixer to beat the butter and sugar until very light and fluffy. Add the eggs one at a time, beating well between each addition.

In a separate bowl, sift together the flour and salt. Fold the sifted ingredients into the butter mixture, alternating with splashes of milk until all are combined.

Grease a pudding steamer well with butter. Place the jam, syrup or chocolate sauce in the bottom. Carefully spoon over the pudding mixture. Cover tightly and lower into a large stockpot of boiling water. Steam for 90 minutes.

Hints & Tips

＊ You can buy pudding steamers from most department stores or online, or better still, look for a second-hand one.

Drunken pina colada mousse

You don't really need to add the rum to this recipe, but it does make it something a bit spesh to serve at a dinner party. It's a bit fiddly, but so worth it!

Serves 6

3 teaspoons powdered gelatine

1 cup crushed pineapple, drained (keep the juice)

½ cup caster sugar

3 eggs, separated

⅓ cup coconut cream

⅓ cup pineapple juice

2 tablespoons white rum

⅔ cup thickened cream

whipped cream, to serve

In a saucepan, bring a 2–3 cups of water to a simmer.

Place ¼ cup of water in a small bowl and sprinkle over the gelatine. Place the bowl in the pan of simmering water and stir until the gelatine dissolves. Cool the mixture to room temperature but don't allow it to set.

Beat the egg yolks and sugar in a small bowl with an electric mixer until thick and creamy. Stir in the coconut cream, pineapple juice, rum and the gelatine mixture. Transfer to a large bowl.

In another bowl, beat the cream until soft peaks form. Fold the cream into the coconut mixture.

Beat the egg whites in a separate small bowl until peaks form, and again fold into the coconut mixture.

Divide the crushed pineapple among four dessert glasses. Pour over the coconut mixture and decorate with whipped cream. Refrigerate for a few hours or until set.

Hints & Tips

✳ A less fiddly way to 'bloom' the gelatine is to microwave it on high for 30 seconds and stir until dissolved.

Drinks

We can't forget drinks, and I'm not
talking about alcoholic ones – although a glass
of wine now and again is good for the soul (but
not in our budget at the moment!).

Flavoured water

Water is, of course, the cheapest drink you can get. Drink lots of it – it is good for you. Some people find it hard to drink enough, so here are a couple of ways to make your water delicious.

Simply add these ingredients to a jug of water and pop it in the fridge for the flavours to infuse:

— a slice of lemon or lime, sliced strawberries or crushed blueberries

— a few slices of cucumber (very refreshing)

— crushed rose petals (very fancy)

— mint leaves and sliced lemon (perfect in summer)

Hints & Tips

＊ Another option is to make up some ice cubes from frozen fruit juice (orange and lemon are great). Then just pop two or three cubes in a tall glass of water.

Teas

Green tea is good for you – drink as much as you like. It is full of antioxidants and the teabags and leaf tea are quite inexpensive.

The cheapest option of all is to make your own herbal teas. Brew a few mint leaves for instant peppermint tea. Grated ginger steeped in hot water is not only delicious but also great for upset tummies. (It's long been used by expectant mums to ease morning sickness.)

Coffee

Iced coffee is great in summer. But how to make it without paying a fortune? One way is to make a coffee, get distracted and remember it an hour later – instant iced coffee, LOL!

Seriously, to make a homemade iced coffee, brew your shot (or dissolve your instant in ¼ cup of boiling water), pour in full-cream milk (it tastes better and is sweeter), add a few ice cubes and enjoy!

Hints & Tips

＊ Obviously, coffee in a cafe is an unaffordable luxury when you're living frugally. If you don't have a coffee maker at home, here's what you can do: place a heaped teaspoon of instant coffee in your cup (plus any sugar if you take it). Now grab a can of creamy evaporated milk and pour in about ¼ cup. Add boiling water and mix well. It tastes amazing – and is a lot cheaper than paying up to $5 in a cafe!

Acknowledgements

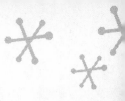

To my delectable husband, Brenny-Poo, who puts up with my 'unique' ideas, zany antics and general bat-shit craziness: thanks babycakes – you are amazing and tremendously good-looking.

Thanks to my two baby boys who aren't really babies any more. You are such naughty little shitters, but I love you to death. Thank you for the constant writer's inspiration you give me, especially with home maintenance and discipline. Please stop wrecking my house.

To Nikkity Nickers, you have been on this whole Stay at Home Mum journey with me, bad sandals and all. You constantly make me cack. Please never change.

Finally, to Rosikins (i.e. Miss Moneypenny): thanks for making sure I adhere to strict deadlines, and for getting my butt into gear. Also thank you for bringing me coffee when required . . . You are a star!

Index

Want to take the stress out of feeding your family?

Jody Allen, founder of the phenomenally successful Stay at Home Mum online community, has the answer for busy mums on a budget. In a single day, cook all your main dishes for a month, freeze them, and then enjoy delicious, nutritious food that is super-quick to prepare when the kids are hungry.

From how to budget for and plan your menus, to how to cook and freeze in bulk, this book has step-by-step instructions and 150 freezable recipes that will save time and money.

You'll wonder how you ever survived without *Once a Month Cooking*!

**Want to put your
money on a diet and save
hundreds of dollars?**

This book gives you the lowdown on spring-cleaning
your finances so you can be frugal while still living well.
Jody Allen, of Stay at Home Mum fame, will help you set
up your household budget, get the best deals, and save
money on everything from your car to your clothes.

And with over 50 thrifty – but fabulous – recipes, you
can be a cost-cutter in the kitchen as well!

**Get sorted and start saving,
with *Live Well on Less*!**